The Book of Alfred Kantor

The Book of Alfred Kantor

An Artist's Journal of the Holocaust

WITH A PREFACE BY JOHN WYKERT

SCHOCKEN BOOKS / NEW YORK

First published by Schocken Books 1987
Originally published by McGraw-Hill Book Company 1971

10 9 8 7 6 5 4 3 2 1   87 88 89 90

Library of Congress Cataloging-in-Publication Data
Kantor, Alfred, 1923–
    The book of Alfred Kantor.
    Reprint. Originally published: New York :
McGraw-Hill, c1971.
    1. Kantor, Alfred, 1923–   2. Concentration
camps in art.   3. Holocaust, Jewish (1939–1945)—
Personal narratives.   I. Title.
NC139.K3A4   1987   759.13   86-27887

Manufactured in Italy
Design by Herb Lubalin
ISBN 0–8052–4029–2 (hardcover)
ISBN 0–8052–0825–9 (paperback)

TO THOSE WHO DIED AT SCHWARZHEIDE

Preface

The Book of Alfred Kantor is sure to be a revelation to those who were too young to have known the events depicted here or to those who did not understand them at the time they occurred. But whatever the previous experience of the Nazi period, one is certain to find in these drawings a young man's indictment that is compellingly contemporary and meaningful right now.

I have had this conviction since 1957 when I first held the original book in my hands. And now that I have helped Alfred Kantor get his book published throughout the world, I also have the opportunity to briefly discuss what I know about the work and the man who created it.

What we have before us is a faithful facsimile of a diary of drawings made by the then twenty-two-year-old "Fredy" Kantor in 1945, right after his liberation from three Nazi detention camps. Even the photos, postcards, and mementos he pasted in his book are included. At the time, a quarter of a century ago, Fredy wanted the world to know what he had witnessed. But then, and for years afterwards, hardly anyone wanted to see or read anything about concentration camps. Consequently, only a few close friends knew about the book's existence. It was not kept secret. But it just stayed in its place of honor on a shelf in the Kantor home in a suburb of New York, as the only part of the past that Fredy had brought with him to a new life.

On occasions I would borrow the book, usually to try and interest someone in its publication. I have been asked why I persisted, despite repeated rebuffs. That is a matter as much of emotional commitment as of intellectual conviction. My motivations—and they are relevant, I think, to understanding the importance of this book—derive from my personal history.

When I was a child I saw Adolf Hitler from the window of my family's apartment. I saw his triumphant entry into Vienna and also felt the terror it inspired that spring of 1938. But luckily in a few weeks I was on my way to safety in America. Months later my family followed. But there were so many, family and friends, who found no refuge. Their plight, in contrast to our good fortune, remains a central fact of my life, more than thirty years after the event.

I had read about the concentration-camp experience, but found it too painful; I could not fathom what it meant to its victims. It was a shock to realize that someone so close to the experience had so little understanding of it. But I really did not know that until I first saw this book. From it I learned that what I had thought too painful to contemplate, the savage destiny of death, was almost incidental or anticlimactic, perhaps even a welcome release from what had already been endured by the concentration-camp inmates.

It seems to me that within the holocaust depicted by this book lurks an even greater horror. Death was not the sting, the preamble of suffering was—the simple systematic process whereby so many human beings were divested of their humanity. This fearful process is amply documented here. It lends the book its chilling historic impact and its contemporary relevance. For the warning is clear: This process is so simple, so easily duplicated, that it can happen again.

But has it ever stopped? There are enough signs and frequent alarms to suggest that, realistically, we must be prepared to fight constantly against the dehumanizing process which continues to appeal to our fellow men. It is not a question of whether the process is starting again; we must content ourselves with the understanding that it is ceaseless; it is not limited to the almost forgotten tragedy depicted here; for dehumanization as a process seems at this time of our development to be firmly rooted in the human condition. Unwittingly, this book is a call to arms. By all means available to us, we must fight dehumanization of any kind, anywhere.

So it is not only the tragic events in middle Europe during the Nazi period that haunt me. My concern is with the present, with the fragility of the human condition and with the effortless ease whereby our savagery reaches the endpoints of what the theologian Harvey Cox has called mankind's persistent refusal to be human. By its protest against naked arrogance, brutality, and violence, this book will make you feel your humanity and that of others. For these pictures bring to mind the words of Bartolomeo Vanzetti. "It is incredible the insult made to the liberty, to the life, to the dignity of the human beings, by other human beings," Vanzetti wrote from his Boston prison cell in 1923. "And it is humiliating, for he who feels the common humanity that ties together all the men, good and bad, to think that all the committed infamies have not produced in the crowd an adequate sense of rebellion, of horrors, of disgust. It is humiliating to human beings, the possibility of such ferocity, of such cowardness."

Similar feelings must have inspired the adolescent Alfred Kantor, who in Auschwitz determined to keep some sort of continuous visual record of what he was experiencing. He had already made some drawings, but for the most part had to trust to memory—there was really no other place to secrete the facts. It had to wait until he was liberated to do as he had vowed. In a two-month frenzy of creation, he filled a book with 127 pages of drawings that distill 1,238 days of his confinement. He was fresh from the ordeal, stirred and indignant, yet joyfully anticipating transportation to a new homeland while still living in a displaced persons' camp in Germany. In the only way he knew, he was also exorcising the emotional scars of the experience.

How amazing that one so young could be so clear, explicit, and dispassionate. The drawings are remarkably precise, even photographic. If the facts are not always exact, it is not because the artist was not scrupulous in his attempt to set down everything correctly. But in 1945 there was simply no way of obtaining the statistics. It is amazing how little has had to be altered in the explanatory text.

Fredy's personal vicissitudes or private feelings hardly ever intrude. He is the meticulous artist, a careful and candid witness who shows what he saw, and, although he is himself involved, refuses to be swept into self-pity. Perhaps because of this reserve, the book's message transcends one personal fate and even the holocaust of the collective Jewish tragedy. There emerges instead a singular indictment of all mankind and of inhumanity at its most unspeakable. And this is achieved without the powers of a Dante, descended into hell, or of a Rouault or Goya, and despite the naive style of the artist and his art.

What was this young man like who not only managed the most difficult feat of the time—that of not perishing—but who also produced this book? Fredy Kantor will tell you that he was very young and perhaps a little too sheltered for his own good. Otherwise he claims being quite ordinary, and just like everyone else. But one does not have to be a close friend to appreciate his special qualities. Much like a twentieth-century Candide, the adolescent was a Parsifal-pure innocent, half-child and half-man. As a victim, he is merely number 168524 in the Third Reich's "final solution of the Jewish question," stripped of everything but his powers to observe. But as an eyewitness, he is a marvel of ruthless precision. This is borne out by the remarkable accuracy of these drawings of remembered events. And being very young, he also maintains a sense of buoyant joy, of adventure: Everything seems possible, even survival. He chooses being over non-being, when to cease to exist may have been easier. He is full of his youth—believing that life is in front of him, certain, somehow, he will outlive the evil he is witnessing. He is willing to laugh at himself, insisting that a youth spent in detention camps does not rule out a sense of humor or an appreciation of the ridiculous. Somehow, he remains irrepressible and undaunted. This may help to recapture the young man; to some extent it also describes the adult.

By the time I met Fredy Kantor, he no longer felt as strong a need to justify his experiences by reporting to the world the unbelievable events that he documented. As a matter of fact, my compelling feelings about having his book published took over while he seemed no longer interested, and was, perhaps, overly concerned that his book would engender new hatreds or rip open wounds that otherwise might have healed.

As I write this in 1971, Fredy Kantor no longer feels the urgency which drove him in 1945. He has concentrated on what he wanted most from life—for what he survived—a private existence which centers on a happy family life. But then, this is how it all had started for him back in Prague, Czechoslovakia.

To a happy, close-knit family, Fredy was born on November 7, 1923. No one suspected that the younger of the two Kantor sons would attain his manhood in the spurious "model ghetto" concentration camp of Terezín (in German, Theresienstadt), the death-camp of Auschwitz, the slave-labor compound of Schwarzheide.

Late in 1941, right after his father died, the eighteen-year-old art student was one of a thousand able-bodied men deported in the vanguard of Czech Jews who were to live in a "showplace" ghetto city. Fredy was part of the work brigades that readied the place for the hordes that were to come, not just Czech Jews, but also those from Austria, Germany, Poland, and other nations. He did not then know that

Terezín, truly a modern tower of Babel, was a ruse. It served as a stopover, and allowed the Nazis to funnel their victims to further deportation or extermination in camps such as Auschwitz, Bergen-Belsen, Lublin, Maidanek, Riga, or Treblinka. In 1943, Fredy was shipped to Auschwitz, but was snatched at the very last moment from the gas chamber. Once again he was one of a thousand workers, this time slave laborers, who worked in an East German factory. Then, just before liberation, he survived a "death march" back to Terezín; of the thousand men "rescued" from Auschwitz, less than 200 survived.

By the summer of 1945, Fredy had finished his book. He then begins to resume his life as if in a headlong rush. He comes to America, returns to art school, and, shortly afterwards, much to his amazement, is drafted into the U.S. Army. In good humor, he comes to terms with life's willful capriciousness. In mock-harshness he rebukes those who gripe that their postwar Army stint is "like being in a concentration camp." To what use does the Army put the recently liberated Fredy Kantor? He plays in the band; his principal instrument, the glockenspiel.

After his discharge, Fredy Kantor again returns to art school, at last finishes his studies and begins to work; he marries a girl who had also been in Terezín and together they raise a family. Today they have a grown son who is studying philosophy and a teenage daughter who has inherited her father's considerable musical talent. As he has for many years, Alfred Kantor works as an artist in the advertising agency where we first met. His spare-time passion is the piano, and his home remains his joy. Careful and steady, the adult has achieved a life he finds both comfortable and satisfying.

Yet, on the great wall in Prague's Jewish synagogue, where the names of 77,297 Nazi victims are listed in tragic and orderly procession, the name of Alfred Kantor appears as one who perished. This was an oversight, Fredy admits ruefully. He wanted to be free, to roam and travel, to have lighthearted adventures, and quickly to start anew elsewhere. So he simply forgot to notify the authorities that he had survived. He knew. Now, because of his book, many more will know and will understand the meaning of his experiences. And that is really all that matters.

John Wykert
New York City, 1971

Since they have dared,
I too shall dare. I shall
tell the truth because I
pledged myself to tell it…
My duty is to speak; I have
no wish to be an accomplice.

Emile Zola: "J'Accuse!"
L'Aurore, January 13, 1898

Introduction

BY ALFRED KANTOR

I drew the pictures in this book at a displaced persons' camp in Deggendorf, Bavaria. I had come there in July of 1945, ten weeks after having been liberated from three and a half years of imprisonment in three Nazi concentration camps. The drawings took about two months from the day a Deggendorf bookbinder had sewn together a book of blank pages for me. With all the impressions of the detention years still in my mind, this was a perfect opportunity to record them in detail.

For some of these watercolors I had as guides pencil sketches actually drawn in the camps. At Terezín, where I was sent first, I was able to draw frequently. As an eighteen-year-old aspiring artist I quickly sought out pencils, paper, and other drawing supplies from people who worked in Terezín's administrative offices. Soon I acquired a notebook, which I filled with sketches of overcrowded life in the dimly lit barrack rooms. I still remember people asking me for a sketch of their bunk, or some other scene of Terezín. Just for a souvenir, they would say, since they expected to return to their previous lives some day and wanted something to show their families and friends.

When I was ordered to leave for Auschwitz in 1943, I entrusted my notebook to a friend who stayed behind in Terezín and who returned it to me after I was liberated. In Auschwitz, pencil and paper were much more difficult to obtain. Yet I managed, for it was here that sketching took on a new urgency. I was determined now to keep a continuous record. Even though I knew there was no chance to take these sketches out of Auschwitz, I drew whenever possible. And, once drawn, these scenes could never be erased from mind. By the time I was deported to Schwarzheide, the third camp, surveillance had become so menacing that I could draw only a little, and most of the sketches I destroyed to avoid being caught. The few Schwarzheide drawings that actually survived did so through the bravery of a friend who smuggled them out.

When I was free again, the rescued material—and

the lost sketches that I had committed to memory—made it possible to put together my diary. The drawings came rapidly but the captions were a problem. I started to write them in my native Czech, but then realized that few people would understand them in America, where I would be living in a matter of months. I decided therefore to write the captions in English, or should I now say in the best Prague high-school English I could muster.

PRAGUE 1938-1941

I was born in Prague, where I lived with my parents, my brother, and my sister in an apartment near the center of town. Mine was rather a happy childhood and adolescence that came to a sudden end in 1938. That fall, at Munich, an independent, democratic Czechoslovakia practically ceased to exist. Soon thereafter, a pro-Nazi government was formed; anti-Semitic signs appeared in shop windows overnight; hate for the Jews began to flourish, fanned by an element among the population that had not dared to surface so brazenly before.

It seemed only a question of time before a full-fledged reign of terror would erupt. The words "concentration camp" were now first spoken at our dinner table. Stories of tortures in neighboring Germany were told in hushed tones. My family discussed leaving the country, but my father became gravely ill and no decision could be made. Soon it was too late to leave, for on the morning of March 15, 1939, the Germans had marched into Czechoslovakia. By September, World War II had begun. I had just enrolled at the Rotter School of Advertising Art in Prague, still hoping to complete a two-year course there. But the Germans ordered the expulsion of Jews from all public and private schools in June of 1940, and I was forced to stop my studies.

The Jewish community of Prague was beset by more and more restrictions. At first one of Prague's most famous cafes was denied them. In a matter of weeks the Germans added movies, the use of parks, and all restaurants. Soon an eight-o'clock curfew was imposed and, before long, Jews were just free enough to breathe the air and to shop for leftovers before the stores closed. By this time my father's illness had reached its final stages. He died just two weeks before I received my deportation notice.

TRANSPORT TO TEREZIN
(THERESIENSTADT)

On December 1, 1941, I reported to the old Fair Building as one of a thousand men who were to be sent to Terezín, an old walled fortress forty miles north of Prague. This group was to convert Terezín from a military post to a settlement for Jews—a supposedly new kind of "ghetto" town. There was some vague impression that it was in my best interest to go; that I would perhaps return to Prague on weekends. The Germans had used every means of reassurance to foster the delusion that all that was involved was a matter of relocation.

I entered the Fair Building, carrying a sleeping bag and enough food for about ten days, just as the mimeographed order had specified. We were told that we were here to be "processed," which meant nothing more than robbing us of whatever valuables we might have. Before daybreak of the fourth day, all thousand of us were marched to the railroad station, half a mile away. The early hour was chosen to prevent our being seen. At the station a special train awaited us, and took us quickly to Terezín (or Theresienstadt, as the old Austrian garrison town was known in German). As the train pulled out of the station, I knew that we were captives of the Germans and that our fate was uncertain.

TEREZIN 1941-1943

Originally, about three to five thousand people inhabited this walled eighteenth-century town, which was two-thirds of a mile long and two-thirds of a mile across. There were over 200 two-storied houses and 14 huge stone barracks. We were billeted in one of the barracks, and contact with the native population was strictly forbidden by order of the SS commandant. Later, when more transports arrived, the non-Jewish residents were moved out, and this baroque town of Terezín was used exclusively as a Nazi concentration camp. Eventually about 140,000

Jews were to pass through, although the most there at any time was about 59,000. These thousands were wedged in—each with about ten square feet of space. Food was terribly scarce, and hunger was rampant. Many of the old and infirm could not endure such misery, and they died within a matter of weeks.

Yet despite the extreme living conditions, Terezín had other aspects which were far less predictable. It was in fact an unusual place, and of all the experiences of my life I find those here the most difficult to describe. For one thing, there was no barbed wire as there was in other concentration camps—which gave at least some illusion of freedom. Also, there were rather few SS men in evidence, as compared to a place like Dachau or Auschwitz. There were times when life even assumed a deceptive normalcy. Many Jews still believed Terezín to be a work camp where they would be safe until the end of the war. There were moments that seemed strangely magnified by a feeling of blissful make-believe amidst an otherwise cold reality. I remember how overjoyed we were one day by the music of an accordion that someone had smuggled into the barracks. Everyone huddled together in the poorly lit, freezing room; and for a while we forgot our hurt as we listened to the tunes. Or I remember how we gathered at night in a cramped storage cellar to watch Karel Švenk's <u>Cheers to Life</u>, Terezín's first underground production. This was a stinging political cabaret, and one of our own men stood guard at the door in case any SS appeared.

And out of small gatherings like these, as the historical record shows, Terezín eventually bloomed (more openly and with little Nazi interference) into a place of recitals, lectures and readings, theatre and jazz, performed by well-known artists, who found themselves here like the rest of us. They all seemed superb to me. No doubt the display of their talents— as long as the Nazis allowed them to perform—eased their own despair and briefly turned Terezín into a small but vigorous cultural center. At the height of its creativity, operas and operatic works were regularly produced, among them Mozart's <u>Magic Flute</u>, Verdi's <u>Requiem</u>, Bizet's <u>Carmen</u>. It was during this period that a remarkable children's opera, <u>Brundibár</u>, was written, staged, and had its premiere performance in Terezín. (I recently heard that it has just been performed in Prague again—twenty-five years after its debut.) There also were several fine string quartets, as well as scores of musicians, singers, poets, actors, playwrights, and painters.

On looking back, it still remains somewhat of a mystery to me how it happened that such performances and such works were permitted. Obviously, the Germans needed at that time to maintain a showplace for propaganda purposes. Eventually, Hitler ordered a film to be made of life in Terezín; now lost, it was entitled "The Fuehrer Donates a City to the Jews." At one point, the Germans even agreed to allow the International Red Cross to inspect Terezín. Blatant charade though it was, it meant some additional comforts: real tablecloths appeared in a newly erected dining hall and the quality of food improved. A cafe was opened and a promenade orchestra performed at the bandstand in the town square. The meadow on top of the fortress—formerly off limits—was now opened for walking and recreation.

All this at the very same time that hundreds were dying within Terezín's walls and thousands were being deported at regular intervals to outlying death camps. It was quite possible for a pianist to be performing at Terezín's city hall at the exact moment that a member of his family was being put on a "transport" to Auschwitz. (In 1942 a railway spur, leading to the center of town, was built by the inmates for the sole purpose of such transports— which meant a trainload of deportees, usually one or two thousand at a time. By 1943 Terezín had become a giant way station, and, ultimately, over 140,000 were sent from this railroad station to their deaths.) Or, while some were promenading in the street, others were being dragged off to the "Kleine Festung" prison, one mile away. Once taken there, few ever returned.

By far the worst memory is of an incident that took place when Deputy SS Chief Bergel called everyone into a large courtyard. He informed us that mail to the outside had been intercepted. (We were not allowed to send letters home then.) If the men who had sent it would step forward within three minutes, they would escape punishment. Bergel fell silent and looked at his watch. Soon nine young men stood there. A week later they were hanged, with the elders of Terezín forced to watch. That night candles were lit in the windows to commemorate the dead and, in some way, as a form of protest. For a time everyone seemed stunned, and these deaths became symbolic of Nazi treachery—they had even greater impact than much larger numbers of deaths later on. Even so, life gradually returned to normal, and I suppose this was the great paradox of Terezín—that life could go on after such brutalities, and that the human spirit found a way to fulfill itself again and even to flourish, at least temporarily.

It was extremely difficult for me to comprehend these stark contrasts. One night, a brilliant cabaret in a cellar; the next, a transport leaving the station. I began to feel the need to record these bizarre scenes, and after a very short time I started to sketch continually almost anything and everything that came to my eye. It was not so much that I wanted to draw my own story, but rather to capture this extraordinary place, so that I could show the world something of it if and when I was ever free.

In May of 1942 my mother arrived in Terezín. She shared a small room with three other women in one of the barracks. That was great luxury, since twenty people or more usually shared a room. I was able to see her regularly, usually after work. Her room was cozy; a large stove in the corner provided heat on chilly days and, more important, a meal could be reheated on it.

By this time I began to consider myself a permanent resident. Hardly any of the thousand men with whom I had come to Terezín nearly two years before had been deported yet. I even had a small circle of friends. Eva Glauber, a girl I had known in Prague, came to Terezín only a few weeks after my mother arrived. For the first time there was enough to eat, since I was working as a stoker in one of the big kitchens that turned out ersatz coffee in the morning and soup, potatoes, and gravy later in the day. I fed the fires under the huge 300-quart kettles. It was a stroke of good fortune to have such a job in the kitchens. Unless you had a job like mine you were hungry most of the time. The small portions from the central kitchens were inadequate. Old people suffered as much as the young, since they were unable to get additional work to supplement their rations. My mother, Eva, and I had an even added fortune. My sister Mimi faithfully sent us food packages. (Mimi had managed to avoid being deported—by being married to a non-Jew.) I also looked for and found a better place to live, a nook under the eaves of one of the houses that could be reached by ladderlike stairs. A friend and I began to convert this place into a cozy <u>kumbál</u>—the Czech word for attic—but I was never to enjoy the planned comfort of this new place.

On September 6, 1943, my mother was one of 5,000 people ordered to leave Terezín as part of a new work brigade in Poland. Two months after her departure I received a card from her postmarked "Labor Camp Birkenau," telling me that she had arrived safely and that all was well. Although none of us knew it at the time, "Birkenau" was the cover name for Auschwitz. Then Eva received her orders to leave Terezín. She had only two days to get ready, and there was nothing to be done but accept the inevitable. I had become close to Eva by this time, and at once I volunteered to join her on the transport. My name was added to the list.

TRANSPORT TO AUSCHWITZ

We were marched to a freight train. Each boxcar held roughly fifty people. As soon as this number was marched up the ramp into the car, the large side door was closed and sealed. Eva and I were to travel in the last car of the train, but by the time it was ready to be loaded there were still ninety people left to be boarded. The guards simply pushed all of us into one car, together with our rolled-up bedding, our rucksacks, and our luggage. As the door slammed shut and was sealed, ninety men and women were standing up in a space hardly sufficient for fifty. It was dark, and only a small shaft of light filtered in from a tiny barred window high up on the side of the car. No one could move a muscle. The prospect of a trip lasting two or three days with our rucksacks on our backs was terrifying. But, fortunately, one young man turned out to be a skillful leader. In a commanding voice he told us to push down all we were carrying to the floor, one by one, then to pile it up slowly so that eventually we could be standing on a solid platform of luggage. The plan worked. Within an hour we had gained sufficient space to move and breathe, although there was no space to lie down. We were still pressed together, but by assuming curiously twisted yoga-like positions, we were even able to sleep. After about thirty hours the train finally came to a halt.

We stood on a siding. Soon we heard muffled sounds, then a loud shouting. The doors of the boxcar were rolled open, one after the other. Finally it was our turn, as a howling of voices descended on us. A voice commanded: "Get out on the double and run to the waiting trucks. Throw away everything and move." Bright lights illuminated the field and husky short men in striped prisoner's clothing used canes to drive, push, kick us down the ramp. The barren ground was frozen and covered with snow. The place was flat and God-forsaken.

AUSCHWITZ 1943-1944

We were herded into an open truck five abreast. I could see through the windshield as the truck careened down a well-lit road with high electrified fences on either side. We passed endless rows of low-slung barracks. Within ten minutes we were being un-loaded by some other prisoners. They stood on either side of the truck's rear gate and directed us to different barracks. Men to the right, women across the muddy road.

Once inside the long, barn-like structure, other prisoners drove us to our new quarters which proved to be triple-tier bunks that seemed to me like over-sized counters and deep shelves in a deserted grocery. Each shelf slept six. One lightbulb, no more than fifteen watts, illuminated the center aisle. It took a while to get one's bearings. Suddenly a voice boomed: "Get into your shelves!" Some half-starved, wild-eyed creatures, dressed in rags, appeared. One came to my bunk and asked if I had any bread left. He did not plead nor did he threaten; he seemed like a zombie, bereft of emotion, yet with an intense expression on his face. Since I still had a small piece, I gave it to him. Then something shocking happened. In a complete frenzy and with incredible speed the boy grabbed the small piece of bread and devoured it. His action seemed inhuman, somehow demented, and I realized as I watched him that people here were not just starving—they were losing their minds.

In the morning the front gates of the barracks were opened. I could see the next barrack, across the street, a piece of blue sky, and throngs of people shuffling in wooden shoes, wearing what seemed like clothes at a costume party. I later learned, but did not know at the time, that these were the redistributed clothes of those who had already died at Auschwitz —coats, trousers, dresses, hats, and shirts arbitrarily assigned regardless of size or fit. After a few hours friends from Terezín who had arrived on the transport before ours found us and were allowed to visit with us briefly. We had not been processed as yet and were informed that we would have to register, that our forearms would have to have numbers tattooed on them and, finally, that there would be a trip to the sauna. Our friends warned us to leave behind all valuables, as we would be stripped of them. They told us that at the sauna our clothes would be taken from us and, like the others who had come from Terezín, we would be issued new clothing.

Almost a week went by before we left the barracks. During that time someone brought a message from my mother telling me where she was, but it was not possible to make contact with her yet. When the day finally came to go to the sauna, I was able to see more of the Auschwitz landscape than I had seen on the first night. We marched in columns of five down the road. It was, I still remember, a cloudy day, as unfriendly and sad as the surroundings. There was neither a tree, nor a bird, just barracks and rows of concrete poles that held the electrically charged barbed wires.

Down the road I noticed a small dark shape lying in the irrigation ditch that ran alongside. At first it looked like a pile of old clothes, thrown into a heap. But as I moved closer, the pile of clothes turned out to be a dead woman, quite elderly, who lay in the ditch. She looked discarded, as one might throw away an umbrella after its metal supports became twisted by a gust of wind. She probably died from exhaustion on the march to the sauna, and the guards must have ordered her thrown in the ditch so she would not block traffic. Further down the road, there were more dark bundles by the wayside. At the sauna itself everything moved quickly. As we had been forewarned, all my clothes were taken away. I was ordered to give up a tiny photograph of Eva I was holding in my hand. We were issued another set of clothes, none of which fitted and which looked peculiar. (Now it was easy for me to understand why the throngs of people I had seen shuffling by on that first morning looked so bizarre.) I received an enormous shirt which had no collar, and which had sleeves that came well over my fingers. This was accompanied by an elegant black velvet vest, but so small that I could never button it. I also received a rather handsome coat with a silk lining that sported a Dutch label. It was a spring coat, although it was now winter in Auschwitz and bitter cold. Everyone was issued a hat. This was the number-one necessity, since regulations required one to take one's hat off for numerous reasons. Mine was strange; it had once been a fine hat but the rim was cut off, except for a small visor-like shape in front.

As soon as I had returned from the sauna, I slipped away and went to find my mother. She had grown thin but not weak. We talked very briefly. In the entire time I was in Auschwitz, I was allowed to see her only occasionally, perhaps no more than eight or ten times. It was easier for me to see Eva, who had come on the same transport and lived in one of the women's barracks across the road. I was not allowed to enter, so I asked one of the women outside to call her. She appeared quickly. We looked at our outfits and Eva thought that we would make a fine pair of scarecrows. In the few minutes we had together I told her how frightened and depressed I was and that I realized that our lives were now in great danger. Although Eva surely knew what I said was the truth she managed to lessen my fears and for the moment to raise my spirits. It was her nature to help others in this way. Even in a time of great crisis she was never beaten down. The strength of her will, and her extreme selflessness, gave hope to those around her.

But whatever comfort I got from Eva lasted a very short time. I became more confused by the hour at Auschwitz. The next day I watched a long column of trucks driving down the main road toward a red brick building about a thousand feet away. They were carrying Jews from Holland, someone told me. Young and old were standing up in canvas-covered trucks. I particularly remember a girl with long blond hair who was wearing a green loden coat. "Soon you will see the smoke; they are done for," said the man next to me. And sure enough, the chimney started up as if for a command performance.

It was chilling moments like these, in the very first days at Auschwitz, that prompted me to find a way to sketch again. Only now I felt obsessed, driven in fact by the overwhelming desire to put down every detail of this unfathomable place. I began to observe everything with an eye towards capturing it on paper: the shapes of the buildings, the insulators on the barbed-wire poles, the battalions of workers at labor sites, the searching for lice, the women carrying soup in heavy barrels, the incredibly eerie feeling of Auschwitz at night with its strange lights and with the glow of flames from the crematorium. At first I began to memorize scenes of the day's activity and then draw them at night in the barracks when no one was looking. It would have been much too dangerous to draw in the open during the day while on a work brigade. Later I was able to draw a bit more freely at the camp infirmary, where Eva was taken when she was striken with tuberculosis. The head of the infirmary, a prisoner himself, risked letting me hide out there and I was able to sketch and draw in the hospital barrack, in a small room not far from Eva's bed. One day I received a gift of a tiny water-color set—I still do not know how it ever got into Auschwitz—from a physician on the sick ward. (A number of Jewish doctors were assigned by the SS to take care of the sick and worked at the infirmary.) He also gave me some paper, and I remember painting small pictures of Prague street scenes for him. The sketches which I had done for myself I tore up as soon as they were finished, but not before I had memorized every line and every figure with the idea somewhere in the back of my mind that I would some day be able to draw these scenes again in order to reveal the true nature of this place.

On looking back, I realize that taking it upon myself to single-handedly "expose" Auschwitz with my drawings could only have come while still very young and while still capable of being so brazen despite the bleakest of circumstances. I realize now, too, that this mission served a much greater purpose: and that was that my commitment to drawing came out of a deep instinct of self-preservation and undoubtedly helped me to deny the unimaginable horrors of life at that time. By taking on the role of an "observer" I could at least for a few moments detach myself from what was going on in Auschwitz and was therefore better able to hold together the threads of sanity.

My first assignment, during January and February, 1944, which lasted for two months, was on a rock gang. We were ordered to carry heavy rocks and stones for miles to help pave the road inside the camp. This was exhausting work, which one truck could have done in a fraction of the time, and many of us—already half starved—became deathly ill. My mother was also assigned to this rock-carrying, and I passed her once and saw her carrying a small stone. About a month later she was taken with all those who had come on her transport to another compound in Auschwitz. The last time I saw her was just before she was moved. The SS planted the rumor that her transport was to be relocated to Heydebreck, a Polish work camp—but actually during the night of March 8, 1944, my mother and all those still alive from her original transport were sent to the gas chamber. (Roughly 4,000 were put to death; about 50, including 10 doctors, were spared.)

After the rock gang assignment I remember a number of odd jobs, such as digging a sewer, splitting rocks with a hammer, latrine duty, and dragging a supply wagon through the camp. The primary purpose of these jobs seemed to be to wear down as many prisoners as quickly as possible. It was only by good fortune that my own strength was not completely depleted. After nearly twelve weeks in Auschwitz I began receiving food packages from Mimi, which regularly included a loaf of bread, a few lumps of sugar, a jar of artificial honey, sometimes margarine and dried fruits. To this day I can offer no conceivable explanation as to why the SS allowed these packages to get through. Without them I surely would have starved. I remember the receipt of my first package. I quickly brought it to Eva, who prized the lemon inside more than anything.

━━━━━━━━━━━

By early June rumors began circulating that those of us who had arrived at Auschwitz in December were at the end of their "six months' quarantine" and would be gassed in two weeks. I thought it absurd that life would just end on one of those sunny June days—quietly and without resistance from us. It seemed terribly unreal. I felt certain that something was about to happen, one more example of the way in which the actualities of Auschwitz were denied. Nor was I alone in fantasizing. Many of us refused to acknowledge what was going on, and false hope was a form of self-protection, a means of preserving one's sanity. For months I was unable to accept the fact that my mother and almost everyone on her transport had been gassed, and I continued to believe the myth that they had been shipped to Heydebreck. The SS, of course, worked hard at fostering such beliefs and were particularly efficient in making the extermination of the Jews a confusing, secretive, step-by-step process. Denial came easily in such an atmosphere, where none of the victims ever had access to the complete plan for the "final solution." Only those on the outside could possibly predict the end result. The majority of prisoners in the camps were face to face with an enemy whose evil intentions they could not fathom, since the Nazis cloaked their designs in promises, ruses, and lies.

By the middle of June, however, Germany began to sustain a series of severe setbacks and the tide of the war had turned. One of their major supply centers of synthetic fuel, an enormous plant in Schwarzheide, was badly bombed. Word apparently came to the SS in Auschwitz that recruits were needed at once to help rebuild it. We were lined up in front of one of the barracks, and those of us who were still young enough and strong enough were singled out— suddenly and unexpectedly we were told we would be shipped out of Auschwitz. The old and the infirm as well as children under sixteen would remain behind and would be destroyed. I immediately became preoccupied with fears about Eva. She had been too sick for too long a time, and I tried not to accept the truth when I heard the news that she did not pass the brief medical examination and had been classified with those who were unfit for work. I was told after the war that Eva was gassed ten days later.

———————

It seemed almost miraculous that after a full five months in Auschwitz I was now being marched down the road with a thousand others and taken to the railroad ramp. We had been issued brand-new blue-and-gray-striped prisoner's outfits and hats. It was a cloudy but balmy day as we made our way out of the camp, passing on our left the gas chamber, a one-storied red brick building with a gabled roof, hidden in a small forest of birch trees. I had a quick thought that perhaps some armed SS would suddenly appear and order us to go in. Maybe the new clothes were just another trick. But the anxious moment passed, and we were soon loaded on a freight train. The German soldier who was guarding us allowed the heavy sliding door of the freight car to be kept open, and we were able to watch the changing scenery on our two-day trip through Poland into Germany.

SCHWARZHEIDE
1944-1945

Our destination turned out to be a cluster of about ten wooden barracks hidden in a stand of fir trees, about two miles from Schwarzheide, a hamlet thirty miles north of Dresden. The camp had housed a detachment of German police, then Italian prisoners of war. When we arrived the Italians were still being moved out. Within 300 feet of the camp was the north gate of the huge factory that had produced synthetic fuels for the German Air Force before it had been bombed. And this, I now discovered, was the reason we had been shipped here—to help rebuild the plant. The sight of severe bomb damage gave our morale a lift; it was our first indication since we had become prisoners that the Germans were not inviolable. My initial impression of Schwarzheide was a relatively good one. The camp was cleaner and airier than Auschwitz. Our new barracks had regular windows and the double bunks were quite comfortable. These minor comforts, however, did little to make up for the fact that from the very first day our workload was unbearably heavy, and that we were to be mercilessly driven by the SS. I remember that one guard shot and killed a prisoner who merely mentioned that his work crew was weak from hunger. Only rarely did any of the guards show compassion, but one actually shared his midday meal with the prisoners under his command. In addition there were German "foremen" to contend with. Some would often become angry and vicious if work had not been done as fast as they demanded, although there was one foreman, named Willy, who treated us as equals. Sometimes he would even hide his lunch sandwich in the tool shack and order a man to go and "fetch that wrench," with a twinkle in his eye.

———

Life was becoming worse here from day to day. I was utterly exhausted after a twelve-hour shift at the plant. Many of the other men became so weak that they neither knew nor cared whether they would survive; ultimately, more than two-thirds of the original thousand succumbed.

My only opportunity to draw came at night in the

barracks, right after what little dinner they gave us, and on Sunday afternoons when we did not have to work. I sketched—and then destroyed—details of the barracks, the gasoline factory, and men at the labor sites. I also sketched the air-raid bunkers which we had been assigned to build.

I had one bit of good luck. Although we were forbidden to write, I was able to get a letter to Mimi because my friend Gerry Velin had the courage to take it to one of the German foremen, who mailed it for us. Within three weeks this foreman brought us a food package she had sent. Later, when we were allowed officially to write home, I began to receive weekly packages. Even more than in Auschwitz these packages were crucial to my survival. Without this extra nourishment I could not have endured the months of hard labor at the factory. Actually, our work proved to be in vain; for the Allies bombed the plant again on August 24, 1944.

During this devastating raid the prisoners were not allowed to take shelter. The plant was reduced to a shambles. One of the bombs hit the barracks across the road and killed many prisoners. Witnessing these deaths tore us apart emotionally; we desperately wanted an Allied victory, yet without shelter our lives were in danger. Every air-raid warning after that sent shivers down my spine. I also became more and more afraid that if the Allies really won the war we would be shot down by the SS, either as a blind reprisal or else to destroy the evidence. I now began to realize that if only we could survive the moment of victory for the Allies, we had a chance of being set free.

That this would become a reality became more and more likely. By March 1945 encouraging news came our way almost daily. One of the prisoners who worked in the SS barrack overheard the Wehrmacht broadcasts and reported them to us nightly. It was now only a question of time before a German defeat. In April we had to build anti-tank traps. Heavy logs were felled and were kept ready to barricade the road should Russian tanks approach. We also had to dig L-shaped foxholes for the German army, which would be lying in wait. These last efforts did not achieve much but our guards were now in a frenzy, driving us even harder than before. At night we could hear the gunfire and see the flashes in the sky. One SS man kept telling us about a new secret weapon that could change things—the V-2 rocket. Nonetheless work at the plant came to a sudden halt, and on the morning of April 18 we were ordered to leave Schwarzheide.

We started south and marched till night fell, having covered almost thirty miles the first day. For the night we made camp in the kiln of a brick factory. The bricks were still warm, as though the workers had just fled. On the next morning, proceeding further south toward the Czech border, we could see dust from exploding artillery shells on the other side of the field we were crossing. At one point we must have been right in no-man's land between the attacking Russian troops and the defending Germans. But compared to the air raids this skirmish seemed far less dangerous. The second night we spent in the barn of a large farmhouse, where a little bit of hot food was served for the first time since the march began. Nevertheless, many men were getting weaker and more and more of them had to be supported, since they could no longer walk on their own. We reached the Czech town of Varnsdorf, which was still occupied by the Germans. There we were taken to a textile mill. It was empty, since the machinery had been removed. We stayed here for almost two weeks with scarcely any food. Some men were picking dandelions and eating them.

At Varnsdorf we were put into open freight cars. It began to drizzle and soon we were all drenched. The food we were given made almost all of the prisoners ill, and many of the weakened men died. After a day's ride the train stopped at a siding in Česká Lípa in northern Bohemia and simply stayed there. It rained even harder now, and more people in the car died. Their dead bodies stayed in the cars with us until the end of the trip. Several German railroad employees, who had become aware of us, tried to obtain permission from our SS commander to serve us their soup. After some negotiation the SS gave in and the railroad men brought it to us. It was a heavenly gift.

In about three days we were on our way again, but only for a few hours. For on the night of May 7, 1945, we had come as far as the railroad could carry us, and much to our surprise we discovered we were now within three miles of Terezín. (I later learned that as the war approached its end, the Germans had agreed to turn Terezín over to the International Red Cross. They also were willing to bring the majority of those left in concentration camps back here. This was actually a token concession on the part of the Nazis, as millions of Jews had already been killed and many died of starvation—as was the case of my own group from Schwarzheide—on their way back to Terezín.) Almost every able-bodied man carried or dragged a weaker man; some died on this last stretch, others barely made it. Of the thousand men that had gone from Auschwitz to Schwarzheide, approximately two hundred were left.

———

In the darkness we crossed the Elbe river and stopped at the gate of the border. The men in the rear were bringing up the sick. I looked for the SS guards. They were well in the back of the straggling column, and they remained there. The gate swung open—this was the border between Nazi Germany and the Protectorate of Bohemia and Moravia. We were on home ground, and the SS men did not cross the border with us.

It was a strange sensation to be suddenly without guards. I felt like rejoicing, yet did not quite dare to, since no one had taken us into custody yet. Suddenly a Czech Red Cross truck pulled up. We were directed to walk to Terezín. Although it was dark and chilly we did not mind at all, and we could hardly believe that we were in familiar territory again. We entered through one of the big gates in the walled fortification and just sat down in the ditch by the road, all of us together. There we sat, stood, or lay and waited. We were inside Terezín now, alive and safe. It was difficult to comprehend that we had survived. I remember how we asked one another what we felt at that moment, as if to make sure that it wasn't just a dream. It was an eerie feeling as we later walked through the place we had been forced to leave seventeen long months ago. It seemed as if an eternity had passed in that time. There were no more blackouts now, and Terezín was ablaze with lights. We were billeted for the night in the town's worst accommodations—the morgue. There were many apologies for this, but we had arrived so late at night that there were no other quarters available. No one cared; we were astonished that someone was apologizing to us rather than bellowing. For the next three days everything that could possibly be done for us was done. We were given food, new clothes, and, most important of all, we were told we were perfectly free to come and go as we pleased.

———

I wanted to return to Prague as quickly as possible. The radio had reported fierce battles raging in the streets between retreating German units and Czech partisans. On the way to the city I saw long columns of disarmed German soldiers, their coats torn, some with rags on their feet. In the villages everyone was out to greet the homecoming men. The town squares and main streets were decked with flags and bunting. Czech women handed out apples, sandwiches, and sweets. I hitched a ride to Prague and got off a short distance from Mimi's house. There were signs of recent street fighting and the nearby Old Town City Hall was a burned-out shell. But the buildings on my sister's street were intact. I hurried up the three flights of stairs to her apartment, where we were reunited.

The first days of freedom were strange. I was so happy to be alive, and at the same time I felt that nothing would ever be the same again. I yearned to roam, to be elsewhere; so I packed my drawings and my sketches and joined a group of ex-prisoners who were going to a displaced persons' camp in Deggendorf, Germany. And it was here that I immediately began to work. Within a matter of days I went to look for a bookbinder. A week later the book of blank pages was ready and I proceeded to fill them, to record what I had seen and observed.

Alfred Kantor
New York City, 1971

-Terezin-
-Auschwitz-
-Schwarzheide-

December 1941 - May 1945

Our new quarters

Terezín: Arrival   Ancient Austrian Fort town
with prison like Casernes —   Our new home

"V" on building walls means "VIKTORIA" — German for Victory

3

70.000 persons living in a small town
    formerly equipped for 3000 soldiers
Temperature   6 above zero centigrade (39°f)
Suitcases are only means securing privacy
of bitterly fought for 6x2 feet plot.

4

THERESIENSTADT: Graben

Old walls and moat surrounding fortress town
of Terezin

Building "flats" on the beds with stolen boards
(appartements)

Theresienstadt, am 20. IX. 1943.

Herrn

Hans Kautor, Prág

Ich bestätige dankend den Empfang ~~Ihres~~ (Deines) Paketes

vom 18. IX. 1943.

Brief folgt.

Fredy Kautor

Unterschrift.

Card sent after receipt of food package
from home.

How to get 70.000 into
city built to accomodate only 3000.

Sick people living below the roof
in clouds of dust

Kitchen for 15.000 persons

food was mostly unnourishing soup,
turnips, rotten potatoes. Young people managed
to swipe an extra turnipe here and there.

serving "dinner"　　　　Magdeburg-Caserne

Old woman trying to get a little extra soup
is being cursed by others waiting in line
for hours. (Kitchens were unable to cook
enough soup at one time)

RAILWAY station

starving people searching
for garbage and rotten
potatoes.

a common view.
Side track into camp was built by inmates
in 1942 to facilitate supply and prevent
prisoners from mailing secret letters at
public railroad station 2 miles away.

9

nejhezčí dvůr

Eva's room

Q 506
Yard where Eva lived
formerly a hotel, now serves as
home to 300.

Czech police searching
for vegetables

Girls working in the „SS-Garden"
were not allowed to pick up even
a single potatoes.

At the border.

Terezín - Southern gate

Czech police, assigned to guard camp, know
well where to look for a swiped tomato
or turnip out of Gestapo gardens.
   Charge was usually: Sabotage on the German
Empire - penalty often death.

11

Serving dinner

Old and sick people had to stand in a queue (line)
for hours. „Dinner" consisting of a clear soup.
was served from 10 - 4 p.m. + potatoes

12

Jewish "police force" "Ghettowache".

The Gestapo ordered all inmates with previous
military service into mock uniforms,
equipped with stick - for interior duties.
In 1943 the entire police force (400 men)
was murdered in the gas chamber.

13

Dentist's ambulance   (Sudeten Barracks)
doctors saved as much as they could,
     worked also for 16-18 hours a day

a busy street   (Hamburg-Barracks)

14

ONE TOILET FOR 1000 people

Due to malnutrition diarrhea and
disenteria where common disoases.
Later latrines were dug

15

TEREZÍNS TYPICAL YARDS.

16

Removal of the coffins to the crematory.
(In summer 1942 220 bodies daily)

EVERYDAY LIFE IN THE GHETTO. PEOPLE LIVING IN SHOPS

Former town stores were converted into living quarters.

Awaiting an international commission

Theresienstadt is "made up" Mock signs are being hurriedly fixed on walls, stores are quickly filled with goods under gestapo rule.

18

This is what the camp looked like when the Swiss Red Cross toured German concentration camps... False Façades, music booth, benches in the park....

Fancy comfort for the commission
(Sick people were sent to death shortly before.
Young and healty had to promenade pretending "a happy life.

"uncle SS Sturmführer" distributing candies
in front of Swiss news-reporter

19

Kaffeehaus Theresienstadt

Ebenerdig

**Eintrittskarte
für das
Kaffeehaus**

am 8. April 1944

Tisch 6

Ticket for Terezín's café

A hidden cultural life developped.
Many inmates were former musicians, singers
actors;

TEREZIN'S CAFÉ
...But smoking is severelly punished

"CARMEN" IN THE GARRET
Bijet's opera accompanied by broken
piano.
Roof had been „Soundproofed "against Gestapo.
with blankets.

20

Plan of Terezín

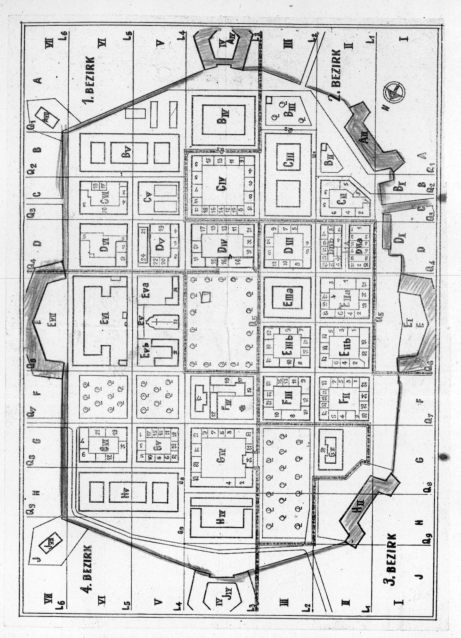

Red line   Brickwall around
the town

DRESDNER CASERNE

Soccer game as entertainment
on sunday

21

Collection of posters

Warning against typhus and appeal for hand-washing
alongside of advertisements for different shows

"play ground" for the commission.
(otherwise a forbidden area)

GESTAPO-PRISON „Little Fortress" half a mile from ghetto.
Czech name: MALÁ pevnost
German name: KLEINE FESTUNG

(Old fort built by MARIA Theresia in 1780 Austrian empress.)

Nobody ever came out alive from here
except a few hundred after Russian army
had liberated town.   23

Einberufung.

s wird Ihnen mitgeteilt, dass Sie weisungsgemass
a den Transport eingereiht wurden. Sie haben sich
reitag, den 12. XII 1943 um 7 Uhr fruh bis langs
 Uhr abends in der Schleuse Lange Strasse 3 ein
ufinden. Nach Erhalt dieser Einberufung mussen S
ofort Ihr Gepack vorbereiten. 2 Handgepackstucke
ax. 30 kg. / Das Gewicht darf nicht uberschritten
erden da diesmal kein Hilfsdienst zur Gepackabgal
lgesetzt wird.

                              TRANSPORTLEITUNG

deportation order

Magdeburg-Caserne
10ᵗʰ of Dec. 1943

Further deportation
menacing

The decision of fate:
List of persons ordered to accompany
the transport into the unknown appears
on the bulletin board of Ghetto H. Q. ... 24.

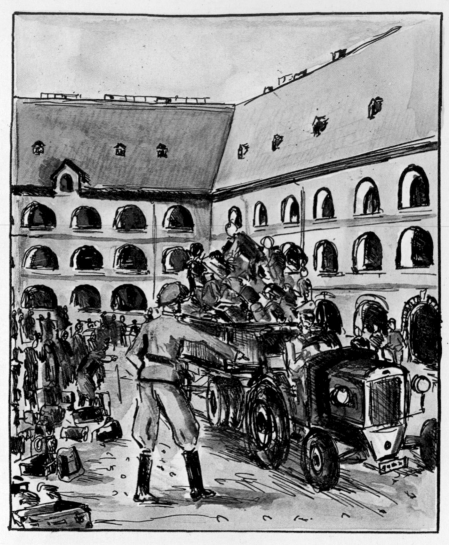

...whose baggage is is loaded already.
Steady influx of deportees brought
figure to 70.000. Germans feared that
diseases might spread and kill their own
people, so capacity was reduced by
shipping inmates to other camps....

"Let's go; hurry up!"

Journey begins

looking for any hint of destination.
And the answer: "Damn fool,...give me your watch,
you won't need it any more!"

numbness and resignation

70 persons crammed in any van
like sardines.
DESTINATION UNKNOWN.

concentration = camp
Auschwitz

arrival   at night   Dec. 18th 1943
after 2½ days in a sealed cattle car...

first thought: what are all the spotlights for,
a movie !

The hell of Auschwitz

Pictures from winter-spring 1944

Throw away all your baggage and hurry
to the trucks!

food., cloth, money and valuables
in the dust...

31

DEC 18 1943

Cross-road of life

...families are torn asunder
by German Super-man...
a move by his finger: immediate death or prison camp. 32

old and sick people, Kids and pregnant women
to death

everybody else By truck to camp „BIRKENAU"
(Vernichtungslager - Auschwitz II)

33

camp Birkenau   Entire view   (20 square miles)

SMOKE OF CREMATORIES, BURNING PRISONERS
AT THE RATE OF 20,000 A DAY* — IN REAR
* IN JUNE 1944

Birkenau   Main entrance
(AUSCHWITZ II)

34

LIFE OF CORPSES

A "greenhorn" asks "What, the hell, is the meaning of this awful smoke!"

35

..while SS is looting our luggage..

IMMEDIATELY AFTER TRANSPORT ARRIVED,
SPECIAL UNITS WERE COLLECTING ALL THE BELONGINGS
OF THE VICTIMS. PART WAS DISTRIBUTED TO GERMANS

Roll-call from 5 in the morning
till night. Our "school" for the future —
CHILDREN AND WIFES IN THE COLD

36

WORKING GIRLS, Their hair cut off

nothing but rain and mud

THE FEW WHO WERE FOUND CAPABLE OF CARRYING OUT
MANLIKE TASKS WERE KEPT IN "WOMEN'S CAMPS". 37
BAR FEETED IN SUB ZERO TEMPERATURE

Electric barbed wire   voltage 500

Try to climb up this fence!

SUICIDES BY TOUCHING WIRE WERE
ROUTINE. BUT USUALLY THE TOWER GUARD
MACHINE GUNNED HIS VICTIM BEFORE IT COULD
REACH MAIN FENCE. POWER WAS USUALLY OFF 38
DURING DAYTIME HOURS.

Everybody has to wear a number

	168.545 / B̲II̲	political prisoner
	168.524 / B̲II̲	Jew
	4.620 / F	~~fancy man~~ "ASOCIAL ELEMENT"
	68.345 / F	professional criminal
	71.403 / A	homosexualist

immediately
after arrival:

Everybody has to deliver all his valuables and clothes
before bathing.

our new "suits"

„Zalezte do regálů!"

vnitřek bloku.

34

interior of barrack

Interrior of a barrack

30 PRISONERS ON ONE TRIPLE DECK BUNK,
BELIEVE IT OR NOT.

Tatooing

Everybody is signed on left arm to prevent
escape.

"Work command, line up "FALL OUT!"

"LABER BATTALION, FALLOUT!"

WHIPPING THE VICTIMS IN THE REAR
IS A FAST WAY TO MAKE A UNIT
LEARN DISCIPLIN. ONE OR TWO TRAMPLED
TO DEATH IS A FINE SCORE

Sunday morning "sport."

It is of advantage to head the group as guard
is in the rear.

LABOR HAD NO USE SINCE THERE WERE
NO ROADS. PRIMARY TARGET WAS TO
WEAKEN THE PRISONERS RESISTANCE.

43

CARRYING ~~Bearing~~ heavy ~~stones~~ rocks.

SS-guard laughs : "What's the matter with you, Lawyer, that's heavier than a pen, isn't it ?"

44

young fellow, age 30
after a few weeks spent in camp

»kapo«

▽ - 8

„the green Eight"
or »The horror of Auschwitz«
(prisoner number 8)

„LÄ" means „Lagerältester"
(camp-leader)

former professional murderer
one of the first inmates
of camp Auschwitz   45

men after hot showers
standing naked in the open air.

46

searching for lice.   (Everyday in the evening)

women carrying „dinner" (turnip-soup)
in heavy barrels

Their dress : blue-striped coats, red head-clothes.

18 year olds looked like 80 year olds.

Serving dinner means a few minutes rest.

Punishment for theft of soup.

49

Absender: KANTOR ALFRED
GEBOREN 4. XI. 1923
BIRKENAU
BEI NEUBERUN
OBERSCHLESIEN.

Rückantwort nur
Postkarten in deutscher Sprache
über die
Reichsvereinigung der Juden in Deutschland
Berlin N 65, Iranische Straße 2

*Fasse
Postkarte kurz!!
am
FERNSPRECHER*

6   6
BERLIN...DIEN...
...DVH5
DEUTSCHES REICH

auf

MiMi MORAVEC

PRAG-V

PHILIPP DE MONTE GASSE 4

PROTEKTORAT

EVERYONE IS PERMITTED
TO WRITE A POSTCARD HOME
INSTEAD OF "AUSCHWITZ"
THE NAME "ARBEITSLAGER BIRKENAU"
HAS TO BE USED.

Scene of hunger

Women carrying "dinner" were allowed
to ~~scratch~~ out barrels after food-distribution.
        SCRAPE
Cold soup and full of splinters but it's

food!

Distribution of supper.

A prisoners ration is a slice of bread daily (250 gram
and twice a week a teaspoon of marmelade,
twice a week a dab of margarine, twice a
week a sliver of salami.

A slice of bread thru the fence.

PRISONERS WIFE, prisoner herself in
adjoining camp helps husband with slice
of bread, saved from own ration.
TOUCHING THE WIRE MEANS INSTANT DEATH.

crematories going on full blast—
a Batch of DUTCH JEWS HAS TO be
disposed of before dawn...

MARCH 1944

Worlds biggest crematory

—From the outside—an innocent
warehouse-looking brick building —
but in the basement: facilities
to slaughter 1000 in 15 minutes....

concentr. camp auschwitz, MARCH 1944

as seen in December 1943 and June 1944

54

Gas chamber

new arrivals don't know the score, and step in
voluntarily, but gassing of veteran prisoners
(usually because they are too worn down for labor)
is combined with screams, and an occasional bullett.

55

transport to death

ϟϟ efficiency : 5 machineguns

for 100 victims...

The Germans are testing war gas
"Cyclone B"....

Ten minutes later.
Prisoners loading dead bodies into trucks.

The gas chamber is the only place where
families stay together....

Gestapo agent looks thro special window
at choking victims.

If there is too much „work" and the crematories
are not sufficient, petrol is poured over the dead
bodies in pits. and they are burnt. Babies
still alive into the fire by order of SS-leader.

"Burning detail" disposing of bodies, never
lived long. But there was more bread ....

58

Gas and oil is transported
on masked Red Cross-vehicles

"Cyclone B"-gas was used.

WORK COMMAND IN THE MORNING

The reminder of the camp is marched
to nearby oil plant. Every evening, weak
men are being selected for the gas chamber.
balloon (Blimp) barrage protecting plant, in
background...   60

8. KOJE – ODDĚLENÍ PRŮJMŮ

"HOSPITAL"

LAST BUNK IN BARRACKS IS FOR
"Disqualifieds" - prisoners weakened
to death. Toilets are behind dead corpses.

61

Loading dead bodies

to crematory

This is a latrine for 10000 persons.
LEFT FOR WOMEN — RIGHT FOR MEN

Sport as punishment.
»Up!-Down!-Up!-Down..!«

"Lets move — pop!"

EFFICIENT METHOD TO GET RID OF OLD PEOPLE.

Sick call—

EVERY TINY SCRATCH RESULTS
IN MAJOR INFECTION, UNDERNOURISHMENT
AND DIRT PREVENT HEALING. ONLY AVAILABLE
MEDICAMENTS ARE CHARCOAL AND TOILETPAPER
FOR WOUNDS.

Suicide : »she went into the fence«

OR : SHE HIT THE WIRE.

A common view in Auschwitz.

40.000 Hungarian women kept in a small camp.
Their children and parents were killed, their
men sent to another camp.

May 1944

Our boys throwing clothes over the wire to the Hungarian girls.

69

A lucky strike:
He got a package!

Dr. Mengele most famous SS Superman.

A motion with His stick and
the victim "passing in review" goes
to his death

Trucks waiting for the victims...

selektion.
naked women **were divided** into two parts.
Keep to right: To work ... or to cremation! (to left)

Victims Have to pass Superman in double time,
weak ones are being sent to waiting truck
to be cremated.

Fettered women to death

disorderly conduct results in death by bullets
Orderly conduct results in cremation.

auschvitz at night

74

July 1   1944

Saved from the hell of Auschwitz
Leaving the „Camp of horror"
After selection healthy boys to work.
into the unknown indeed, but far away from the "chimney"
Our women stay behind to be gassed
two days later····

75

July 1 1944 – April 18 45

66566

Schwarzheide

numbers are issued upon
arrival, to be worn on shirt
and also on trousers

AFTER 2 DAYS OF STARVATION
IN SEALED FREIGHT TRAIN:

DESTROYED GERMAN GAS MANUFACTORY
NEEDS HELP

JULY 1, 1944

Original sketches done in Schwarzheide

ARRIVAL AT THE NEW CAMP.
— WILL IT BE ANY BETTER HERE?

CAMP COMMANDERS TOAST UPON ARRIVAL:
"YOU DIRTY RATS! I'LL SHOW YOU WHAT A CONCENTRATION CAMP
REALLY IS! SoYou think you have been places?..."

Arrival at Concentration camp Schwarzheide

JULY 1, 1946

5 A.M.

View from "Autobahn" Berlin-Dresden.
Camp on the right

Barrels on the left are Smoke screen
apparatus To Hide area during AIR RAID.

SS-Unterscharführer's hobby

JUMPING ON A MAN'S INTESTINES MAKES HIM FEEL MERRY.

barbed wire around the camp

LABOR BATTALION
» ~~Work=command~~, line up! «
passing the gate in the morning
ON WAY to PLANT

Cojsme koupili?

.. WHO'S WITH US TODAY?

(GUARDS WERE CHANGED DAILY,
SOME 5-10% WERE PLEASANT
FELLOWS.

» Hello boys, be carefull, today the redhaired guy is guarding us!

(DON'T TURN AROUND WHILE THEY'RE BEHIND US! –)

Gasoline manufactory „BRABAG"

84

Line up!

(-"SIR, 20 PRISONERS PRESENT

FOR DETAIL AND ACCOUNTED FOR")

("HERR POSTEN 20 HÄFTLINGE ZUR ARBEIT ANGETRETEN!")

85

"LET'S GET A MOVE ON"

A WHIP IS AN ESSENTIAL MEANS OF
SPEEDING UP PRODUCTION

Building anti-air raid forts

— 110 LBS OF CEMENT ON YOUR BACK
AND 800 CALORIES PER DAY
IS A SHORTCUT TO THE CREMATORY

"HURRY UP, GENTLEMEN, WILL YOU ?"

(A DERAILED LORRY—
2 BROKEN LEGS)

(DAILY SCENE WHILE BUILDING
AIR RAID "FORTS" FOR THE NAZIS)
(ABOVE GROUND-SHELTERS

GUARD IS GONE

GUARD COMES BACK

88

Permanent dream of a c.c. prisoner.
"Food, food, food...... nothing but food!!"

89

"Dinner" is served by prisoner-"superman"
in the courtyard of factory
Usually you receive your soup and a strike
in the face (instead of dessert)

CALORIES { NEEDED - 3000
{ RECEIVED - 500

90

ARTIFICIAL FOG IS USED TO HIDE THE PLANT
BEFORE ENEMY PLANES

BARRELS ARE SET AFIRE SOME FIFTEEN MINUTES
BEFORE ALARM IS SOUNDED

PLANT DISAPPEARING BEHIND
SMOKE SCREEN. (LUCKILY, HIGH CHIMNEYS
WILL LEAD B-17 TO THEIR DESTINATION
ANYWAY)

ALARM IS SOUNDED

ROAR OF PLANE FORMATIONS CAN BE HEARD.

DANTE'S INFERNO- A POOR COMPARISON!

RED BALLOONS (PAINTED BARRELS
ARE OPTICAL AIR RAID WARNING

Get away quickly & our heroic guards
are gone already. FOG PREVENTS
FROM BREATHING— SEEING

IN THE AIR SHELTER

MAN IN FRONT DIRECTS US
TO DUCK (AS IF IT WOULD HELP...)
AS NEW WAVE OF B-17 APPROACHES...

95

THE PLANT IS BEING HIT
BEAUTIFULLY,
SOON THE WAR WILL BE OVER...

SIGN BOARD READS:
"NO SMOKING — INFLAMABLES!"

also synthetical gas burns okay.

96

BOMBS!

— PRISONERS HAVE TO STAY
INSIDE THEIR BARRACKS.

("JUST HOW MUCH CAN A
WOODEN ROOF WITHSTAND? —
A MESS GEAR AND CHAIRS
GIVE US PROTECTION FROM FLYING
SPLINTERS

bombs are crashing!

AUGUST 24, 1944   12:30 pm

DIRECT HIT INTO BLOCK Nº 1.

98

SURVIVORS OF THE RAID RUSH TO
THE BURNING PLANT

99

FIRSTRATE WORK OF B.17
STEAM IS HISSING FROM TORN PIPES
LIKE A DYING DRAGON

100

LOADING UNEXPLODED BOMBS—
A PRISONERS JOB

101

» WHEN THE CAT'S AWAY   THE MICE PLAY «
(a guards conversation with a German girl... "it means
a few seconds rest for us)

102

BRITISH AND U.S PRISONERS ARE BEING EVACUATED
FROM EASTERN GERMANY DAY BY DAY
AS RED ARMY ATTACKS COTTBUS
(January 1945)

KNEE BENDS

A FEW PUSH-UPS WILL PROVE
IF MAN CAN STAY ON DUTY
OR HAS TO BE SENT TO THE GAS CHAMBER.
PRISONERS' NUMBERS ARE BEING TAKEN —
AND CALLED OUT AT THE NEXT ROLL CALL

104

"BAUSTELLE 19"   OUR WORKING PLACE
FROM SEPT. UNTIL JANUARY 1944

105

ROLL CALL IN THE EVENING

PRISONER NUMBERS OF DISQUALIFIED
MEN ARE HOLLERED BY FOREMAN.
IT MEANS DEATH IN THE GAS CHAMBER
IN BERGEN-BELSEN

106

NIGHT SHIFT (6PM - 8·AM
DECEMBER 1945

BUILDING AIR RAID SHELTER

AT 5° -ZERO

107

GARBAGE - OUR TREASURE

IN THE BACKGROWND - SHELTER
BUILT BY PRISONERS.
(SMOKE STACKS BEAR CAMOUFLAGE COLOR) 108

Schutzhäftling

Alfred Isr. K a n t o r
geb. 7.11.1923   Nr. 85.566
Block:Schwh.

K.L. Oranienburg

Inhalt: 1 Brot
          4 St. Kuchen
          1 Päckchen Grammeln
          1 Stück Speck
          1 Tiegel Fett
          1 Tiegel Marmelade
          1 Apfel
          3 Eier
          6 Stangen Würfelzucker
          1 Wurst
          1 Paar Wollsocken
          1 Paar lange dunkle Trainirhosen
          1 Päckchen Pastillen gegen Durchfall

Abs.:Mimi Moravec
     Prag I., Phil de Monteg.4

A package from My sister!

SUNDAY MORNING IN THE CAMP

(THE LAST 2 MONTHS IN SCHWARZHEIDE
ARE SOMEWHAT. EASIER — BUT
FOOD RATIONS HAVE BEEN CUT 50%) 109

DININGROOM* HAD EVEN STOVE,
CHAIRS, TABLES.
   * OFF LIMITS DURING DAYTIME

110

FELLOW PRISONER HIDES UNDER
THE "ORDERLY ROOM'S" WINDOW, LISTENS
TO GERMAN BROADCAST, TAKES NOTES
FOR SECRET DISTRIBUTION TO
HIS MEN.—

111

IN THE LAST MOMENT SS GUARDS
FORCE US TO BUILD ANTI TANK TRAPS.

GERMAN FOXHOLE IN FORE GROUND.
TO BE USED FOR NEW WAPON "PANZERFAUST"

112

RUSSIAN FRONTLINE APROACHES!
LINE UP FOR EVACUATION   APRIL 18, 1945
5 A.M. - APRIL 18, 1945

THE DEATH MARCH BEGINS ON THE FIRST DAY: 25 MILES

(OUR GUARDS ARE JUST AS TIRED, ONLY BETTER FED)

FLEEING GERMANS

APRIL 19, 1945

114

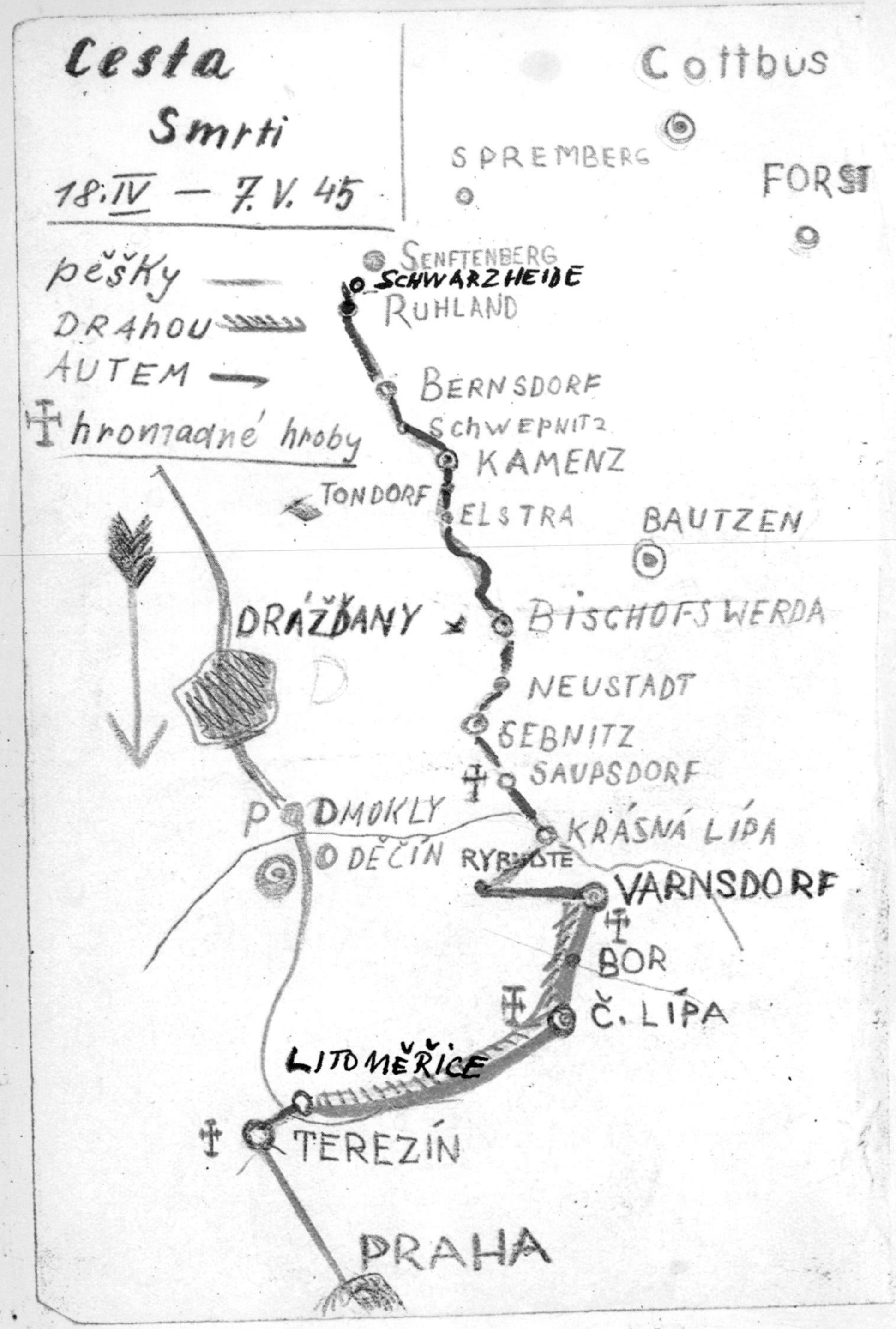

Cesta Smrti
18. IV — 7. V. 45

pěšky —
DRAhou ⊩⊩⊩⊩
AUTEM →
✝ hromadné hroby

Cottbus

SPREMBERG

FORST

SENFTENBERG
SCHWARZHEIDE
Ruhland

BERNSDORF
SCHWEPNITZ
KAMENZ

TONDORF ELSTRA

BAUTZEN

DRÁŽĎANY

BISCHOFSWERDA

NEUSTADT
SEBNITZ
✝ SAUPSDORF

KRÁSNÁ LÍPA

PODMOKLY
DĚČÍN RYBNIŠTĚ

VARNSDORF
✝ BOR

✝ Č. LÍPA

LITOMĚŘICE

✝ TEREZÍN

PRAHA

80 miles ON FOOT: SCHWARZHEIDE — VARNSDORF
60 miles BY TRAIN: VARNSDORF — LITOMĚŘICE
36 miles BY TRUCK Terezín — PRAGUE

CAMPING IN THE RAIN

BISCHOFSWERDA
APR. 20, 45

GUARDS STACK ARMS
AND BUILD CAMP FIRE, WHILE
PRISONERS JAM TOGETHER TO KEEP WARM
IN INADEQUATE CLOTHING

115

APRIL 23 1945

CROSSING FORMER CZECHOSLOVAKIAN BORDER
NEAR KRÁSNA LÍPA
(AT THE MOMENT
IT IS STILL CALLED) SUDETENGEBIET)

DEAD BOYS ARE PILED UP ON CARS.   APRIL 21, 45

(THE SS TROOPS APPARENTLY HAVE
ORDERS NOT TO LEAVE ANY TRACES
OF THEIR ATROCITIES....)

WEAK MEN ARE SHOT DOWN ON THE ROAD.

LAST REVENGE OF THE GUARDS CHIEF.
HANGING FOR ESCAPE.
MAY 1 1945 NOON

PRISONERS HAVE TO LOOK ON —
— ANYBODY TURNING FACE TO THE GROUND
IS WHIPPED BY S.S. FUEHRER

STARVING ON OPEN VANS IN ČESKÁ LÍPA   MAY 6/7 1945
SECOND VAN REPORTS: SIXTEEN MORE DEATHS
AND TEN DYING OF COLD AND HUNGER.

GUARD IS STILL ON HIS POST.
MAROONED FOR DAYS IN THE RAIN — NO ENGINE IS
AVAILABLE. FRIENDLY GERMAN RAILROAD MEN
ARE ALLOWED TO FEED US HOT SOUP. AFTER
SS CHIEF GIVES IN TO THEIR REQUEST TO HELP.

UNLOADING THE DEAD BODIES AT LITOMĚŘICE.

S.S. MAN YELLS : "EVERYBODY OUT !"

121

OUR GUARDS LEAVE US TO OUR FATE AN FLEE
AT 11 p.m. ON Czeck border near.....
.........Teresienstadt!!

WE CAN'T BELIEVE IT — ITS OVER! 122
(175 OUT OF 1.000 ARE ALIVE)

RED CROSS TRUCK
APPEARS — BUT CAN'T TAKE
175 MEN.   WE SPEND THE
NIGHT ON THE ROAD — BUT
IN A DREAM.... IT'S OVER!

123

TEREZÍN MORGUE—
our first night free is spent here

A BATTERED GROUP DRAGS
IT'S FEET TO A SHELTER.

HOUSES ARE JAMMED WITH LIBERATED
PRISONERS TO CAPACITY
SOON AFTER A TYPHOID FEVER TOOK HUNDREDS OF LIVES

124

A OPĚT, TEREZIN

91

SOME PEOPLE NEVER HAD TO
LEAVE THERESIENSTADT — NOW
THEY GIVE US FOOD AND CARE.

MY FIRST MEAL: BARLEY BROTH
AT LEAST $\frac{1}{2}$ GAL.

WE STILL CAN'T BELIEVE, IT'S REALLY TRUE!

SAVED IN THERESIENSTADT!

Girls, who have been in lucks way during wartime
and could stay in T. care for us affectingly.
many of our old friends cannot recognize us.   125

May 10, 1945

126

10.V. 1945

CZECH PEOPLE FEED US AT EVERY PASSING
VILLAGE, KISS US AND THROW FLOWERS
ALL OVER THE HIGHWAY.

Happy End

Notes

Facing

Page
2   As of September 19, 1941, no Jew over the age of six years could appear in public without a "Star of David" firmly sewn on his outer clothing above the heart. By police decree, this "identification badge" consisted of a black six-pointed star on yellow material, as big as the palm of a hand. In the center was the inscription "Jew."

Page
2   Prague, December 1, 1941: Trolley number 17 at the Fair Building, about one mile from the heart of Prague. It was from this stop that the deportees walked a short block to the old Radio Fair Hall, the processing center in which they would remain from four to ten days before being taken to a concentration camp.

Page
4   Our first quarters were several large storage areas on the third floor of a huge eighteenth-century military barrack, the "Sudentenkaserne." We were crowded into limited space, and each man put the mattress he brought from home on the damp and cold cement floor, with his baggage and belongings ringed around for an illusion of privacy.

(top)
Page
5   Within a few months, men assigned to the carpentry shop built triple-decker bunks to squeeze in as many people as possible. Each bunk slept two men. Strangely enough, a large amount of good lumber was found here at a time when even a single board was unobtainable in Prague. Some of the men on the carpentry detail managed to steal a board or two.

(bottom)
Page
5   Although strictly forbidden, a few inmates managed to construct a cozy home-away-from-home on the top of the bunks. Usually the two men who shared this enclosure nailed a board to the sides for privacy and improvised curtains, a shelf, a table, arranged mattresses to form an L-shaped couch, and even put up a drawing.

Page
6   By late 1942 Terezín was filled to capacity, with old people even crowding the attics. Often these attics had to be reached by a steep climb up a ladder. These were dark, dusty places where loose floorboards and hard-to-see beams made it difficult to move around. For the old, the sick, and the ill-fed, this was part of the great hardship of Terezín. To let a little light into the gloom of the attics, some people would knock out a few roof tiles. But then, whenever it rained, they

had to put a bucket underneath to catch the water.

Page 9 The railroad depot proved to be the easiest place for scrounging an extra potato, a turnip, or even a lump of coal dropped during the unloading of a train. This depot was at the end of a two-mile spur built by the inmates of Terezín in 1942 to connect to the Berlin-Prague line. Now supplies could be shuttled in and out of the camp without being observed and, as I later realized, Jews were taken secretly from this depot to death camps in the East.

Page 10 One of Terezín's typical courtyards. The small house on the right was formerly a hotel. Eva Glauber lived in the house with the balcony. Addresses consisted of the alphabet letters followed by numbers. For instance, Q506 stood for avenue Q, fifth street, house number 06.

Facing Page 10 These pencil sketches were done on the spot in Terezín. The bottom one, showing the room Eva shared with five other girls, was made in Terezín in 1943. The girls with the help of their boyfriends had dressed up their rooms with shelves, a little table, and stools, a lampshade, and drawings on the walls. One of the boys on the carpentry detail made the convertible beds which in the drawing are folded away for the day.

Page 11 Czech policeman searches a girl inmate. Some of Terezín's women were assigned to work in the vegetable fields outside of the camp. On returning from work, they were searched for any stolen onions and potatoes hidden in their clothes. Being caught and reported to the SS could sometimes mean early deportation from Terezín to Auschwitz.

Page 13 The Ghettowache (literally, ghetto watchmen) were Jewish prisoners assigned by the SS to guard public and private property. The ranks of this internal security force came from a few hundred of Terezín's earliest inmates who were promised exemption from further deportation. But later, I believe sometime in 1943, the entire force was disbanded on the spot and sent to Auschwitz when an SS commander pointed out that it might be risky to keep a cadre of well-trained Jews in the camp who might form the nucleus of a possible revolt. Their place was soon taken by older, weaker men.

(top) Page 14 The dental clinic was in the barrack in which I lived. It served all of Terezín's inmates, and some of Prague's best dentists were on the staff. ("Ambulance" is the Czech word for outpatient clinic.)

(bottom) Page 14 One of the main thoroughfares in Terezín, with railroad tracks visible. The building at the left center is another barrack, the Hamburg Kaserne. The other buildings were former private homes. All of them built in an eighteenth-century manner, they were not allowed to be higher than the outside city wall.

Page 17 A wagon loaded with coffins made of raw wood. Because of the great number of elderly people who were subjected to cold, hunger, and other hardships of Terezín, this wagon and others like it were a familiar sight. Many many old people died of "natural" causes, actually due to the privations they were forced to endure. The death rate rose so high and so rapidly that eventually a crematorium was built, since graves could not be dug fast enough.

Page 18 Curious, even mystifying, improvements were undertaken by the authorities of Terezín. A barbershop opened, the sign read Frisör, German for barber or beauty shop; a drugstore appeared several weeks later. What up to then had been a police station became a bank for Terezín inmates who were handed "ghetto bank notes." The park was readied for band concerts and a children's playground. Finally, a coffee house opened, and a jazz group that had been practicing furtively now played openly in the cafe. The fixing up, the prettifying, and the future promise of all sorts of amenities amazed everyone in the drab and overcrowded camp.

All this activity was soon explained. An International Red Cross Commission was expected, and arrived after I left Terezín. But much of the freshening up and redecorating was done while I was still there. I learned later that the sham was carried through without a hitch. The foreign visitors were shown a pleasant, smiling Terezín, well stocked with goods that people could buy with their money; older persons strolled in the park where benches had been placed; young people played soccer; decent food was served in a mess hall. The "model ghetto" with its Jewish self-government was an illusion fostered by the Nazi captors. Supposedly, a few members of the Commission were taken in by this outward display, but the moment they left most of the improvements disappeared.

(top)
Page 20 For us who were so young at the time, Terezín was hard to understand. Here was acute suffering, constant hunger, and unbelievable human degradation. And at the same time there were attempts at human dignity. Terezín's coffee house symbolized this valiant striving for a remembered aspect of the life led before the Nazis came.

It was not a regular cafe like the many which had existed in Prague. No food was served. However, attractive waitresses wearing black dresses and white aprons served ersatz coffee in real china cups. There were tables and chairs, and the walls had been decorated by a number of Terezín's fine artists. All this was in sharp contrast to life outside of the cafe, where people often lacked a pot or a messkit, where a table and a chair were considered great luxuries.

The main attraction at the cafe was a small jazz group, The Fricek Weiss Jazz Quintet, the Ghettoswingers. They played daily, but one was allowed to visit the cafe for only two hours about once a year. Nonetheless, such a visit was an unforgettable experience. I knew while I was there that this was not a true coffee house which one could leave to go home to one's family or friends. There was no gossip or laughter. People sat quietly, some with tears in their eyes while they listened to the music. For each of us it was two hours of escape, of make-believe.

(bottom)
Page 20 The stage was set for a Terezín performance of Carmen.

Facing Page 21 Plan of Terezín, designed by the Technical Office in the Magdeburg Barracks.

Page 21 Soccer was played by those young men who had sufficient strength. A game was started as soon as a ball was found. Actually, shortly after we arrived, a pair of goal posts were put up in the courtyard of our barracks. At once the SS Chief ordered them removed, and we assumed that this ended any further possibility of playing. But the SS did not interfere with subsequent attempts at soccer, as they no doubt wanted to foster the illusion of Terezín as a model ghetto. The games were now allowed in the court-

yard of the Dresdner Barracks, but because of the small size of the yard the teams had to be reduced. For those who watched, the view was good from the barrack's many balconies. The SS men would also watch, but to us it did not matter. We were young, and we enjoyed the Sunday afternoon games which brought so many people to this courtyard for a few hours of relaxation.

(top)
Page 22 Posters appeared everywhere in Terezín; at first timid and small, they grew bolder and bigger. This was one more Nazi device for making Terezín a so-called "cultural center." In a movie of life in Terezín, which has now been lost, much was made of the announcements of cultural events in the midst of official exhortations to wash one's hands or to guard against typhus.

(bottom)
Page 22 This playground was right on top of the city wall. The bastion had been spruced up for the visit of the International Red Cross Commission. It was off-limits a good deal of the time, but on days when inmates were permitted access, this was one of the nicest spots in Terezín. Beyond the battlements, one could see the neighboring hills and the fertile countryside.

Page 24 The list of deportees posted at the ghetto headquarters in the Magdeburg Barracks. The fear of deportation gripped everyone. Days of despair and frenzy preceded each departure. Often a transport would tear a family apart. A son would leave his parents behind or, as in my case, my mother would leave before I did. Worse than this, no one knew where the freight cars were heading. I had been in Terezín for two years when Eva and I received our deportation notices.

Facing Page 24 Deportation order: The following notice was personally handed to the prospective deportee and read: "This is to inform you that you are to join this transport, as per order of the camp authority. You are to report on Friday, December 12, 1943, from 7 a.m. but no later than 6 p.m. to the transport staging area at Lange Strasse 3. You are to proceed immediately after receipt of this order to prepare your baggage (2 pieces of hand baggage—total weight 30 kilograms max.). This weight is not to be exceeded, as there will be no help to assist during baggage collection for this transport." — **Transport Department**

Page 25 SS man supervises loading of baggage. Deportees were permitted sixty-five pounds of soft baggage, rucksacks, and bedding tied into a roll. These had to be brought to a central collection point near the railroad depot.

Page 26 Cattle cars were drawn up on the railroad spur that led directly into Terezín, and during December two transports, each carrying 2,500 people, left the camp and headed East. Our train consisted of about thirty-five two-axle freight cars. They were rather small and at best could hold about fifty people. Yet seventy people were marched into each car, and ninety were crammed in the last car of the train to which Eva and I had been assigned.

The only source of air and light were tiny windows on the top of the car which were effectively barred by wires. Because of the overcrowding, we were all pressed against each other. Panic and hysteria was averted only by the quick and clear thinking of one of the men who took charge and ordered us to work the baggage we were carrying down to the floor so that we would be standing on it. We were still scarcely able to move, but somehow we did manage the thirty or more hours of our journey East.

Page 33 Our entire transport was herded into trucks and taken to a compound. Ordinarily new Auschwitz arrivals were divided into two groups by an SS officer. The strong and healthy were told to walk to their new quarters a short distance away. The others were taken immediately to their deaths.

Page 34 Auschwitz (Oswiecim) was the biggest of the mass-murder factories. The black smoke from the crematories was visible everywhere, but at the beginning of my stay I had no idea what it meant. Only later was I to learn that this was the place where some two million were murdered.

Though distorted somewhat, this view of Auschwitz shows the two rows of sixteen barracks in each compound as well as the main road leading to the crematories.

Auschwitz actually consisted of two sections or camps. The old one was called Auschwitz I and had brick barracks. In 1942, I understand this was a concentration camp for political prisoners that contained about 15,000 inmates. By April 1944 the number of prisoners was 180,000. In the adjoining camp called Birkenau, the barracks were of wood, and there were four crematories. Birkenau was the address our captors insisted we use when we were allowed to write home. Our return address did not read "Concentration Camp Auschwitz," but "Work Camp Birkenau."

Page 35 The dead were carried to the loading area behind one of the barracks. Naked and dirty corpses were carried like boards.

(bottom)
Page 36 We were ordered to stand in front of the barrack every morning and wait for the roll call. Only two SS men counted 10,000 of us. This often took two hours or more. When the roll call was completed, we were marched to the rock pile. In May of 1944 a man escaped. On that day we stood roll call all day, being counted over and over again. (As it turned out, an SS man had helped the prisoner to escape.)

Facing
Page 39 Each prisoner, both Jew and non-Jew, was ordered to wear a number tag preceded by variously colored triangles. Red triangles signified political prisoners; green, professional criminals; black, "dodgers" or labor slackers, and "antisocials"; pink, homosexuals; violet, members of Jehovah's Witnesses (Bibelforscher, in German). All Jews in my compound wore a red triangle to signify that they were political prisoners and a yellow triangle inverted on this to signify that they were Jews.

Page 39 On the third day, we were taken to the sauna, or showers. (The sign reads Unclean Side.) As we entered, we had to divest ourselves of everything. This made certain that we did not have a single photograph or a tiny good-luck charm left. After the showers, we all received something to wear. These clothes belonged to former dead prisoners and rarely fit properly. Furthermore, for the raw winter of Auschwitz, our warm clothes had been taken away and instead we were issued mostly summer-weight clothing.

Page 40 An inside view of our barrack. Each one was about twenty feet wide and some 120 feet long, with construction rather reminiscent of horse stalls with small windows overhead.

In triple tiers, wooden shelf-like bunks lined the sides of the building. A brick duct, about two feet square, extended down the center of two-thirds of the barrack. At both ends the ducts led into brick ovens; one sometimes had a fire going so that hot air would warm the bricks of the duct. But our barrack was unheated, since a low fire in one oven is all we were allowed. I used to visit a friend at the dispensary, because I could sketch there for a time during the spring of 1944, so I knew that the two ovens were capable of providing sufficient heat.

Page 43 The road which was being built by the prisoners was being rolled by this giant roller, pulled by fifteen men. An SS man walked behind them, supervising. The road was never finished, not even after six months of work. Two trucks could have done the labor of 10,000 prisoners in a few days, but that was not the Auschwitz way. The prisoners had to be worn down.

Page 51 The section leader (Stubenaeltester) distributes supper. He spread a blanket across the heating duct and prepared the portions for about forty-eight men. We received a piece of bread, about 250 grams (5/8 of a pound), and three times a week we were given a one-ounce slab of margarine; twice a week a spoonful of beet marmalade; once a week a very thin sliver of salami, or a small piece of Hartz cheese. Supper was served after the evening roll call, sometime around six or seven P.M. For lunch we had a quart of soup, usually made from turnips. Breakfast consisted of some sort of watery unsweetened tea. This diet was insufficient to sustain a working man for more than a few months. Without some supplementary food, death from malnutrition was certain.

Page 52 During May of 1944, when thousands of Hungarian women occupied the adjoining camp, the guard towers separating the two compounds were left unmanned and it was possible to approach the wire barrier during daytime hours. This picture shows a man and his wife at the barrier. She is giving him a portion of her ration.

Page 53 I will never forget this surrealistic scene of nighttime Auschwitz. The pale lights from the barrack windows made me think of a miner's camp, peacefully asleep. In stark contrast, a bright flame shooting out of a low smokestack, a thousand or so feet away, instantly brought back the reality of the camp. Black smoke billowed from the chimney, for during the nights of May and June 1944 thousands of Hungarian Jews were being killed. The flames burned night and day for weeks. At other times there were occasional days of respite from the flames; they would flare up on one night, and would be quiet the next. After the war I learned the true statistics of those days and nights. The number of Hungarian Jews murdered in Auschwitz and Treblinka has been estimated at 250,000 to 400,000, and 20,000 people were gassed and cremated in one single night of June 1944.

Page 54 One of four crematories in Auschwitz. This crematory was a long, low brick factory building with a window in the attic and a high-gabled roof. Its surroundings were clean and cheerful. I remember seeing a small cluster of trees near the building, and lots of shrubs around its walls. A sign near the entrance to the gas chamber said, "To the Disinfection." The door to the gas chamber was at the side of the building; death and destruction were under one roof.

Page 55 On the way to the sauna, I was able to look into one of the gas chambers. The door stood open, since the gas chamber was not in operation at that time. All was quiet; the room's gruesome purpose could not be guessed. It was perhaps 800 feet square, with a low ceiling. It was dark inside; the little windows did not let in much light. I was amazed to learn after the war that up to 2,000 people had been gassed at one time in one of these chambers.

Page 59 Poison gas containers were transported to the gas chambers in vehicles disguised as German Red Cross ambulances.

Page 60 Around six every morning we could see a long column of prisoners, flanked by their guards, marching to work. They were accompanied by a band that played the same rigid and metallic-sounding version of the popular wartime polka, "Roll Out the Barrel." This happened every morning.

Page 61   The last row of the bunks was reserved for the sick or those near death. The man on the left, down to perhaps seventy-five pounds, supports himself as he slowly shuffles down the corridor in order to sit near the stove on the warm brick duct. It was hard to sit up on the top bunk, nearly impossible in the lower ones. The two boxes at the right with their lids open are toilets, exclusively used by the sick who were unable to get to the latrine which was situated about 700 feet away.

Page 62   Every morning those who had died during the night were placed on the floor near the area reserved for the sick. Later they were removed to a collecting point near one of the barracks. From there a crew of prisoners piled the corpses on a wagon and took them to the crematory.

Page 64   Our entire barrack near the end of the compound served as a latrine for both sexes. It was also used as a hiding place when prisoner-overseers (the Kapos) were looking for workers. Everyone tried as best he could to preserve what little strength he had. Therefore, the latrine was most crowded just before assembling of work details in the morning. Often the Kapos' first stop was at the latrine to chase out "shirkers."

Page 65   Forcing the prisoners to do knee-bends or push-ups was a pastime enjoyed by the SS guards and even by the Kapos. The slightest infraction of a camp rule, such as being caught with a hat on inside the barrack, was frequently punished by making the entire barrack exercise in the mud. Often a prisoner's weakened condition led to his collapse in the field or to his death.

Page 66   At the far end of the barrack, near the brick oven, a primitive dispensary was set up nightly after supper. The prisoner-medic, usually a physician, did his best but could not provide the most urgently needed medicine—food. All he had was charcoal for diarrhea and tissue paper for bandages. He could do nothing for the malnutrition that caused boils and infections which refused to heal.

A dispensary barrack, where prisoners received somewhat more elaborate care, was at the end of the compound. Admittance was limited strictly to those suspected of having an infectious disease, such as scarlet fever.

Symptoms of ordinary starvation or a life expectancy of a few weeks were too commonplace to warrant medical care.

Page 67   An accident, not a suicide. A girl prisoner who had spotted a friend among a newly arrived group in an adjoining compound tried to reach something through the wire fence. For some reason the power, always turned off during the day, was on. The girl died instantly. She had been very popular, especially in the children's quarter where she worked. Why and how this happened was never explained. But there was a formal inquiry into her death. This was done at a time when thousands of people were gassed and cremated in a single night.

Page 68   The Hungarian women who survived the "selection" for death at their arrival suffered intensely in the next compound. They were constantly screened by SS doctors to see who should next be killed. At the sauna, their hair had been cropped short and they had been robbed of all their possessions. They were dressed in rags and froze in the chilly Auschwitz nights, since they had no blankets. There was no water in the barrack, which was shared by more than a thousand women, about twice the amount of people housed in other barracks.

Page 69   The men of our barrack threw bundles of clothing to the Hungarian women. After six months at Auschwitz we had acquired a few extras, some blankets and some clothes. Also, because the barbed-wire fence that separated the two compounds was not being guarded during this period, we were able to go near the fence. Previously this had been forbidden, and guards would fire at anyone who approached the fence. We managed to communicate with the women across the fence as best we could, so that short-lived friendships blossomed across wire barricades. We learned that they had been separated from their husbands and children; and they did not know about the gas chambers.

Page 70   I received food parcels in Auschwitz, about one a month while I was there. They had been sent by my sister, who was married to a Christian and thus could remain in Prague. These parcels sustained me. Each contained a loaf of bread, some cookies, an apple, sugar cubes, and even some sausage. I never quite understood the reason why food parcels were permitted by the Nazis.

Page 71 Nazi Dr. Mengele. He was responsible for thousands of deaths. He conducted monstrous experiments on inmates, and frequently took charge of the selection process that separated the new arrivals into those who were put to death immediately, and those who were allowed to live briefly.

Page 75 By a stroke of luck I was chosen to leave Auschwitz during the sixth month of my stay there. It was a time when it seemed certain that I would be gassed, since few inmates lived longer than six months in Auschwitz. But the order came that those still strong enough for work were to be moved to a German labor camp. First we had to get showers and be processed. After that we were to board a train.

Page 77 After several days on a train we arrived on a siding deep within some pines. We were met by an SS guard unit and marched along a road which led by a huge factory complex. It seemed to have been damaged recently by air raids. I was somehow convinced we were close to a major city, a comforting thought after the desolate location of Auschwitz. But actually the Braunkohlen-Benzin Allgemeine Gesellschaft (Brabag, for short) was built in 1938 deep within the woods, ninety miles south of Berlin and thirty miles north of Dresden on the Berlin-Dresden highway or Autobahn. The plant was a major producer of synthetic fuel. It had been successfully camouflaged until shortly before we arrived when Allied bombers had discovered the place.

Facing Page 78 .These little pen-and-ink sketches were done in Schwarzheide, as part of a booklet of the same format. Five of these sketches from the booklet appear in this book.

Two weeks after our arrival in Schwarzheide I was asked by some fellow prisoners to draw a few scenes describing life in our new camp. Later the sketches were bound into a little book, which was to be given to the Lageraelteste, the camp elder. He was a prisoner also but, as a German, he was sent from another camp to Schwarzheide to take over the post of prisoner-in-charge. The gift plan was abandoned, after the men found out that the Lageraelteste was not worthy of their attention. Another prisoner, Julius Rabel, hid the drawings under a floorboard in his barrack. Later on the death march he kept them on him and safely brought them home.

Page 78 We were brought to a small camp hidden among pine trees. There were a dozen small wooden barracks in a pleasant setting about one mile from the main gate of the Brabag plant. The first impression was favorable. We were 250 miles from Auschwitz, but it seemed as though we were really far, far away from the horrors of that death camp. Here the barracks had real windows; there were even flower beds. This had been a prisoner-of-war camp and some Italian POWs were still being evacuated as we arrived. A devious-looking SS man introduced himself as our new leader. While everyone stood at attention, he motioned to a man in prison garb to make the welcoming speech. This man was a political prisoner. He was to be directly in charge of us and would act as a sort of liaison between the SS and the prisoners.

Page 79 The barrels on the left side of the Autobahn are fog-making devices. Before an air raid a spray of white mist from the many nozzles could engulf the factory area in a blanket of thick fog within minutes. This was aimed at preventing the Allied bombers from spotting their target.

Page 80 Blaeser was the sadistic SS man in charge of the Schwarzheide slave-labor camp. He carried a thin bamboo rod that he used to whip prisoners while they stood lined up in formation. This habit earned him the name Rákoska, Czech for cane.

Page 81 Building this barbed-wire obstacle for about 1,500 feet around the camp was my first assignment at Schwarzheide. The SS was concerned that the existing fence was inadequate and wanted to make sure that the camp was "escape-proof."

Page 82 Work details left the camp each morning for the mile-long march to the Brabag factory. Each man in the group — they might number from twenty to a hundred — carried his own mess bowl under his arm. Everyone was forced to do heavy manual labor, except the barrack head (the political prisoner), barrack orderlies, kitchen personnel, and those who were ill. SS guards accompanied each group, two for small ones, although as many as six SS men would guard the large work details.

Page 85 The prisoner foreman (<u>Vorarbeiter</u>) had to click his heels and report to the SS guard that his men were ready to work. This happened when we arrived at the plant. Usually a German foreman would then take over. The latter were sometimes decent men, though some were as brutal as the SS guards. They drove us to the edge of our limited physical endurance.

Facing Page 86 A giant cement mixer had to be fed without interruption. Men carried 110-pound cement bags on their backs, practically running to avoid a lashing by the guards. The fresh cement was poured continuously into the foundation of the air-raid shelters. In six months, eight of these massive, bomb-proof shelters had been erected.

Page 90 Noontime soup distribution was followed by a twenty-minute rest period. Like the Auschwitz diet, Schwarzheide's rations were insufficient to sustain life unless supplementary food could be obtained. Black unsweetened ersatz coffee was available at breakfast, and dinner consisted of a bread ration slightly smaller than in Auschwitz. A thin slice of salami or a dab of margarine was provided. Part of the bread ration was held back and issued in the morning, and was eaten during a work-break at nine A.M. The noon meal was invariably turnip soup or some equally undernourishing brew. On Sundays, a day during which we worked until two P.M., the food was a little better—a few potatoes with a tasty sauce. These rations for death were part of the solution of the Jewish problem planned by the Nazis. Throughout their domain Jews were allowed only a fraction of the rations allowed Germans or conquered nations. They were allowed bread, potatoes, and sugar but no meat at all, and no fat. And where a German or a Czech was allowed almost six pounds of bread a week, a Jew was allowed only one pound.

Page 91 An irritating fog that was the sign of future victory. In the summer of 1944 almost every clear day would bring an air-raid warning at around eleven in the morning. Shortly before the appointed hour, tension would grip guards and prisoners alike. As the numerous barrels began spraying a fine mist that soon turned to a pea-soup fog, we knew that an air raid might be due shortly. We listened to the wail of the sirens, since this was also our signal to leave the plant and march back to the camp. We were pleased by that, as it indicated that the fortunes of war were turning against our captors. The constant air raids were a strangely frightening forerunner of good news. One could now entertain the fantasy of possible liberation.

Page 93 As soon as the air-raid warning was sounded, all civilian workers left the factory as quickly as possible. Many had bicycles, others jumped on departing trucks and buses. The vehicles headed for the woods—a safe distance from the target area. Only the Jewish prisoners were not allowed to seek shelter; they were hastily marched back to their barracks, where they were forced to remain during the raid.

Page 94 In addition to the sounding of the sirens, two red barrels were hoisted to the top of the water tower as soon as an air alert was announced.

Facing Page 95 The original of the pencil drawing done in Schwarzheide immediately following an air raid. It shows the prisoners who were allowed, for the first time, to enter a shallow shelter during a raid. They are seen ducking in anticipation of a bomb burst.

Page 96 During the raid on August 24, 1944, the plant was damaged so severely that fuel production was halted completely. It had barely been restored when another major raid, six months later, wrecked the factory again. We feared these raids, having to face the bombs without shelter, but we also knew that they were a neccessary part of an Allied victory.

Page 98 During this raid a bomb hit barrack No. 1, which was crowded with prisoners. There were many deaths and scores of wounded. The camp had no facilities to treat the casualties.

Page 99 Right after the "All clear" signal all prisoners were marched into the burning plant for rescue and fire-fighting. One group had to separate burning tank cars from a string of those which were not on fire. Others had to repair railroad tracks torn up by bombs. All this had to be done quickly. We were forced to work all night in addition to the regular day shift.

Page 100 On the day after the raid, destruction was so extensive that it looked as if not a single barrel of synthetic fuel would ever be produced at Brabag again. Steam escaped from burst pipes, twisted girders pointed to the sky in grotesque shapes, debris was piled up on the roads, and the plant was pockmarked with craters.

Page 101 Unexploded bombs had to be loaded onto trucks after having been defused by a German bomb expert. Some of the bombs had dug deep into the sandy soil and were hard to find. Work on the bomb squad was the most hazardous assigned to prisoners.

Page 103 One day in January of 1945, while working outside the usual work confine of the factory, we saw a long stream of war prisoners being led by Wehrmacht men. We were astonished to see American and British war prisoners. Their evacuation gave us the first hint of the Russian offensive in East Germany.

Page 104 After the evening roll call one day prisoners were told to do one kneebend each when their turn came to step forward. This unusual order by the SS chief was nothing but a physical test of each prisoner's condition. By the time this test was made, several months after our arrival in Schwarzheide, many men had become walking skeletons. As each man's prisoner number was noted the list of undesirables grew. On the next day this group was shipped to the Bergen-Belsen concentration camp. None returned.

Page 105 For five months, from September 1944 to January 1945, we dug excavations into which gasoline tanks were to be buried. The colored brick walls hid other tanks. Camouflage color was painted on the wall to hide it from aerial observation.

Page 106 Roll call was held twice during the day. In the morning before the march to the plant began, and at six P.M. immediately after returning to camp. Prisoners stood five abreast, the smallest man first, the tallest last. An SS man quickly paced down the ranks counting off each row. As soon as roll call was over, the command Weggetreten (dismissed) was given. Evening roll call was the time when those who looked unfit for further work were observed and their numbers taken down.

Page 107 Men of the night shift built an Elektrobunker, a special air-raid shelter, to house the power plant. It was a solid concrete block, some forty feet high, in which electrical equipment (the heart of the factory) was to be kept safe and operating during air raids. Night shift started at six P.M. and lasted until about seven or eight A.M.

Page 108 The structures in the background are the air-raid shelters we built. The walls were many feet thick and the rounded shape of the roof was supposed to deflect a striking bomb. Many prisoners had lost their lives building these monstrous constructions. Most of them collapsed from hunger and weakness.

Page 109 Two men carried a thermos full of black coffee to their barrack every morning. In March of 1945 the fierce tempo of work began to slacken, as if the Germans were beginning to feel the end was near. But at this time our food rations had been cut in half. I was one of those fortunate ones who were able to receive food packages. My sister Mimi in Prague kept sending them, hopeful that at least some might reach me. The packages arrived intact. Without a doubt these packages saved me and some of my friends from starvation.

Facing Page 109 A list of the contents had to accompany every food package that came from my sister Mimi. The one shown here contained: 1 loaf of bread; 4 pieces of cake; 1 package of pork rinds; 1 piece of bacon; 1 jar of fat; 1 jar of jam; 1 apple; 3 hardboiled eggs; 6 small packs of sugar; 1 piece of sausage; 1 pair of woolen socks; 1 pair of dark lounge pants; 1 package of dysentery pills.

Page 110 Half of the barrack was turned into the company room. There we could sit after roll call was over. We just ate our ration at the tables, and those who had received a package could now fetch it from the barrack leader, who kept the food packages locked away during the day. Soon after we had eaten we went to sleep in the adjoining part of the barrack, where double-tiered rows of wooden bunks stood.

Page 111 One of the prisoners had access to the SS men's barrack, which had a radio.

During the last months of the war he supplied us daily with the latest reports from the battlefields. After work he made the rounds from barrack to barrack, where he repeated the news and even added his own analysis of the war situation. In this fashion we learned of the Russian advance in the East and of the crossing of the Rhine at Remagen by the Allies.

Page 112 In a last effort to stem the tide of advancing Russian troops, the SS hastily made us build anti-tank traps. We had to fell heavy trees and carry the trunks on our shoulders to the roadside, where foxholes were dug. The tree trunks were to be used as roadblocks. They were placed in a vertical position to be lowered across the road when enemy tanks approached. A Panzerfaust (German type bazooka) would then be fired at close range by a member of the Volkssturm, a quickly organized posse of old German men.

Page 113 On April 18, 1945, we were ordered to evacuate Schwarzheide. It was clear to everyone now that the Russians were very near. About a week before this day we had been to the factory for the last time. It had been bombed repeatedly, but I was amazed at the tenacity of the German foremen, who carried on with iron determination as if nothing had changed. Yet Germany was, by then, in its death throes.

When the evacuation started, fifty men of the first group to leave were harnessed to a special gear and pulled a small wagon loaded with some food supplies and the supplies of the accompanying guards.

Facing Page 115 The death march. This is the map of our entire trip from Schwarzheide to Terezín. Prague is at the bottom southeast of Terezín. The total distance is about 150 miles. Eighty miles from Schwarzheide to Varnsdorf were covered on foot, about forty miles from Varnsdorf to Terezín by train, and the rest (roughly forty miles) by truck.

On the first day of our evacuation march we met wagon trains of German refugees. They were fleeing before the advancing Russian army. All their belongings were on the wagons. From their rugs they had fashioned colorful roofs. At first glance we were reminded of a traveling circus.

We were not told where we were headed, but from casual observation we could tell that we were moving in a southerly direction, toward the Czech frontier. On the first day we covered twenty-five miles on foot. Men were dropping from exhaustion, some died on the road. We bivouacked in an abandoned brick factory, its ovens still warm as if the workers had only left hours before we moved in. The next day we marched further south, losing more men. On the fifth day of the march we still did not know what our final destination would be.

Page 116 We are now crossing from Germany proper into Nazi-occupied Czechoslovakia. It took some five days to reach Varnsdorf, in the northernmost tip of Czechoslovakia. We had, by now, covered eighty miles on foot, bearing south from the onset of the march zig-zag fashion, dodging the advancing Russian troops by a few miles, in one instance by the length of one football field.

Page 117 As our men kept dropping from exhaustion, the stronger ones tried to drag them along but the SS men stopped them. Dying men were loaded on the wagon and carried for some distance until they could be buried.

Page 118 At some points along the route the chief SS man shot some prisoners who could not keep up with the march. Today memorial plaques with the names of the executed men are on the exact spot where they had been killed.

Page 119 In Varnsdorf we were kept in the empty machine hall of a textile mill for almost two weeks. We hardly received any food anymore and grew weaker by the day. One day the SS chief hanged a prisoner in full view of everyone. The prisoner had been caught while trying to escape. We were forced to face the execution.

Page 120 We suffered miserably in the open freight cars. It rained all the time and we were soaked, sitting in puddles of water. Before we had left Varnsdorf we had all eaten a yeasty-tasting spread, hungry as we were, and we did not notice that it had not been fresh. On the train everybody became ill. Men started dropping from food poisoning; this in addition to their weak condition killed a large number. After several hours and traveling twenty-five miles we arrived at Česká Lípa station, where we were shunted to a siding and forgotten. The cars just stood there for two or three days. Many prisoners died. During the last day at the Česká Lípa station some German railroad workers requested permission from our SS commander to serve us their soup. When they were allowed to do so, it was the first drop of food we had gotten since Varnsdorf. Finally an engine came and the trip continued. It was on this last stretch that I was told by fellow prisoners that we were to be returned to Terezín, the ghetto we had left seventeen months ago. It seemed possible. I knew the countryside the train was passing, and we were, indeed, headed in the right direction. We could hardly believe that we would come to Terezín again. We thought the SS would probably bring us to the Terezín fortress, the Kleine Festing Gestapo prison, near the ghetto.

Page 121   After a few hours we had covered twenty-three miles, and the train pulled into Litoměřice (Leitmeritz). Now we knew for sure we would be going to Terezín, since it was only two or three miles from here. It was nighttime when we arrived at the station and began to assemble for the last stretch. With our last burst of strength we helped the weak, carried them or pulled them in every conceivable way to make sure that they would survive this last obstacle.

Page 122   When we came to the Czech border we knew that a dramatic moment was near. Our guards, who had been with us on every step up to now, turned around and stayed a short while in the rear of the column of prisoners, which wound its way across the border. Then they disappeared back towards Germany.

We could hardly believe that we were free. It had come so unexpectedly after the grim days in the train, with so many men dead just before the end. After a short walk up the road, which we all knew from the past, we just sat down in a ditch and waited. Out of a thousand able-bodied men, who had been shipped out of Auschwitz a little over nine months ago, only 200 were left. The remainder had died from overwork and starvation.

Page 123   While we stood on the highway, unsure what to do next, a truck came by. The driver urged us to walk to Terezín, which was only a ten-minute walk from there. After forty-one months of constant fear we felt utterly confused and, somehow, strangely abandoned. We walked the distance in a loose formation. The return to the ghetto was a powerful, emotional experience. It was about eleven P.M. as we walked through the cobblestone streets. All houses and all barracks were jammed with people.

We were given emergency quarters in the morgue, as it was too late to find better accommodations, but we were too excited to mind this minor inconvenience. (The morgue had been empty and we slept as best we could on some old furniture, which stood about, mostly chairs, sofas, or plain boards on the stone floor.)

Page 125   News of our middle-of-the-night arrival must have spread quickly, as the first group of Terezín girls was there to greet us shortly after sunrise. They brought food, blankets, even chairs to make us comfortable. Later many more people came; they all stayed with us till nighttime, caring for the sick and cheering us with the latest news of the Allies' victory.

Page 126   I remained in Terezín for two days to receive new, clean clothes. (My prisoner's suit I discarded, after having removed the number tag for a keepsake.) On May 10 I boarded a truck provided by the quickly set-up Czech repatriation committee, and left for Prague. There were signs of recent battle on the highway and some detours had to be made around blown-up vehicles blocking the road. As we approached the first town on our trip south towards Prague, women were gathered on the road and handed us food, flowers, and blew kisses. This happened in every village and town on the forty-mile trip. Colorful bunting had been installed across the highway; everyone must have been preparing for this day, the day after VE day. Russian vehicles were following our truck, and soldiers, still in their winter coats, threw cigarettes and candy to the population, who cheered them in turn.

Page 127   Back in the center of Prague, one day after VE day. (May 10, 1945.) The flags of France, England, Russia, and the United States flew at full staff. The picture shows a returned former prisoner, still in his striped suit, talking to people around him.